BURTON ON BURTON

Burton on Burton

Edited by
Mark Salisbury

Foreword by Johnny Depp

faber and faber
LONDON · BOSTON

First published in Great Britain in 1995 by
Faber and Faber Limited
3 Queen Square London WCIN 3AU
This paperback edition first published in 1997

Photoset by Faber and Faber Limited
Printed in England by Clays Ltd, St Ives plc

A CIP record for this book is available from the British Library

ISBN 0-571-17393-4

4 6 8 10 9 7 5 3

Contents

To Jo, with all my love ...

Acknowledgements

The major part of the interviews for this book were conducted during one week in April 1994 in New York, where Tim Burton was in post-production on *Ed Wood*. These were supplemented by a number of subsequent interviews which took place in the months leading up to the film's US release, as well as material from two previous interviews with Burton, the first in 1990 while he was in London filming *Batman*, and the second in Rome in 1991 when he was engaged on a promotional tour for *Edward Scissorhands*.

I would like to thank Tim Burton for his time, patience and enthusiasm for this project during a particularly demanding period of time. Thanks also to Jay Maloney, and the staff of Tim Burton Productions – especially Eva Quiroz – for all their help and assistance.

Many many thanks to Johnny Depp for his perceptive and informative introduction, and for their assistance in making it possible I would like to entend my gratitude to Tracey R. Jacobs, Christi Dembrowski and Stephanie A. Johnson.

I am also indebted to Denise Di Novi, Scott Alexander and Larry Karaszewski, Alan Jones, Kim Newman, Phil Thomas, Tony Timpone, Michael Gingold, Jaime Tucker, Michelle Sewell, Angela Smith, Emma Cochrane and Jeremy Clarke, and for their support and guidance, Walter Donohue and Kevin MacDonald.

And finally, many thanks to Sue Bond for her truly miraculous travel agency skills ...

Stills appear courtesy of BFI Stills, Posters and Designs and Alan Jones. Copyright for the stills are held by the following: the Walt Disney Company Inc. (*Vincent, Hansel and Gretel, Frankenweenie, Tim Burton's The Nightmare before Christmas*, and *Ed Wood*); Warner Bros (*Pee-Wee's Big Adventure, Batman*, and *Batman Returns*); Amblin Entertainment (*Family Dog*); The Geffen Company (*Beetlejuice*); and Twentieth Century Fox (*Edward Scissorhands*).

Illustrations appear courtesy of Tim Burton.

Foreword

In the winter of 1989, I was in Vancouver, British Columbia, doing a television series. It was a very difficult situation: bound by a contract doing assembly-line stuff that, to me, was borderline Fascist (cops in school ... Christ!). My fate, it seemed, lay somewhere between *Chips* and *Joanie Loves Chaachi*. There were only a limited number of choices for me: (1) get through it as best I could with minimal abrasion; (2) get fired as fast as I could with slightly more abrasion; (3) quit and be sued for not only any money I had, but also the money of my children and my children's children (which, I imagine, would have caused severe chafing and possible shingles for the rest of my natural days and on through the next few generations of Depps to come). Like I said, this was truly a dilemma. Choice (3) was out of the question, thanks to extremely sound advice from my attorney. As for (2), well, I tried and they just wouldn't bite. Finally, I settled on (1): I would get by as best I could.

The minimal abrasion soon became potential self-destruction. I was not feeling good about myself or this self-induced/out-of-control jail term that an ex-agent had prescribed as good medicine for unemployment. I was stuck, filling up space between commercials. Babbling incoherently some writer's words that I couldn't bring myself to read (thus having no knowledge of what poison the scripts might have contained). Dumb-founded, lost, shoved down the gullets of America as a young Republican. TV boy, heart-throb, teen idol, teen hunk. Plastered, postered, postured, patented, painted, plastic!!! Stapled to a box of cereal with wheels, doing 200 mph on a one-way collision course bound for Thermos and lunch-box antiquity. Novelty boy, franchise boy. Fucked and plucked with no escape from this nightmare.

And then, one day, I was sent a script by my new agent, a godsend. It was the story of a boy with scissors for hands – an innocent outcast in suburbia. I read the script instantly and wept like a newborn. Shocked that someone was brilliant enough to conceive and then actually write this story, I read it again right away. I was so affected and moved by it that strong waves of images flooded my brain – dogs I'd had as a kid, feeling freakish and obtuse when I was growing up, the unconditional love that only infants and dogs are evolved enough to have. I felt so attached to this story that I was completely obsessed. I read every children's story, fairy tale, child-psychology book, *Gray's Anatomy*, anything, everything ... and then, *reality* set in. I was TV boy. No director in his right mind would hire me to play this character. I had done nothing work-wise to show that I could handle this kind of role. How could I convince this director that *I was Edward*, that I knew him inside and out? In my eyes, it was impossible.

A meeting was set up. I was to see the director, Tim Burton. I prepared by watching his other films – *Beetlejuice*, *Batman*, *Pee-Wee's Big Adventure*. Blown away by the obvious gifted wizardry this guy possessed, I was even more sure that he would never see me in the role. I was embarrassed to consider myself as Edward. After several knock-down-drag-'em-outs with my agent (thank you, Tracey), she forced me to have the meeting.

I flew to Los Angeles and went straight to the coffee-shop of the Bel Age Hotel, where I was to meet Tim and his producer, Denise Di Novi. I walked in, chain-smoking, nervously looking for the potential genius in the room (I had never seen what he looked like) and BANG! I saw him sitting at a booth behind a row of potted plants, drinking a cup of coffee. We said hello, I sat down and we talked ... sort of – I'll explain later.

A pale, frail-looking, sad-eyed man with hair that expressed much more than last night's pillow struggle. A comb with legs would have outrun Jesse Owens, given one look at this guy's locks. A clump to the east, four sprigs to the west, a swirl, and the rest of this unruliness to all points north and south. I remember the first thing I thought was, 'Get some sleep', but I couldn't say that, of course. And then it hit me like a two-ton sledgehammer square in the middle of my forehead. The hands – the way he waves them around in the air almost uncontrollably, nervously tapping on the table, stilted speech (a trait we both share), eyes wide and glaring out of nowhere, curious, eyes that have seen much but still devour all. This hypersensitive madman *is* Edward Scissorhands.

After sharing approximately three to four pots of coffee together, stumbling our way through each other's unfinished sentences but somehow still understanding one another, we ended the meeting with a handshake and a 'nice to meet you'. I left that coffee-shop jacked up on caffeine, chewing insanely on my coffee-spoon like a wild, rabid dog. I now officially felt even worse about things because of the honest connection I felt we had had during the meeting. Mutually understanding the perverse beauty of a milkcow creamer, the bright-eyed fascination with resin grapes, the complexities and raw power that one can find in a velvet Elvis painting – seeing way beyond the novelty, the profound respect for 'those who are not others'. I was sure we could work well together and I was positive, if given the chance, I could carry out his artistic vision for Edward Scissorhands. My chances were, at best, slim – if that. Better-known people than me were not only being considered for the role but were battling, fighting, kicking, screaming, begging for it. Only one direc-tor had really stuck his neck out for me and that was John Waters, a great outlaw film-maker, a man both Tim and I had huge respect and admira-tion for. John had taken a chance on me to spoof my 'given' image in *Cry-Baby*. But would Tim see something in me that would make him take the risk? I hoped so.

I waited for weeks, not hearing a thing in my favour. All the while, I was still researching the part. It was now not something I merely wanted to do, but something I *had* to do. Not for any ambitious, greedy, actory, box-office-draw reason, but because this story had now taken residence in the middle of my heart and refused to be evicted. What could I do? At the point when I was just about to resign myself to the fact that I would always be TV boy, the phone rang.

'Hello?' I picked up.

'Johnny … you are Edward Scissorhands,' a voice said simply.

'*What?*' flew out of my mouth.

'*You are Edward Scissorhands.*'

I put the phone down and mumbled those words to myself. And then mumbled them to anyone else I came in contact with. I couldn't fucking believe it. He was willing to risk everything on me in the role. Head-butting the studio's wishes, hopes and dreams for a big star with estab-lished box-office draw, he chose me. I became instantly religious, positive that divine intervention had taken place. This role for me was not a career move. This role was freedom. Freedom to create, experiment, learn and exorcize something in me. Rescued from the world of mass-product, bang-'em out TV death by this odd, brilliant young guy who had spent his youth drawing strange pictures, stomping around the soup-bowl of Burbank, feeling quite freakish himself (I would learn later). I felt like Nelson Mandela. Resuscitated from my jaded views of 'Hollyweird' and what it's like to not have any control of what you *really want* for yourself.

In essence, I owe the majority of whatever success I've been lucky enough to have to that one weird, wired meeting with Tim. Because if it weren't for him, I think I would have gone ahead and opted for choice (3) and quit that fucking show while I still had some semblance of integrity left. And I also believe that because of Tim's belief in me, Hollywood opened its doors, playing a strange follow-the-leader game.

I have since worked with Tim again on *Ed Wood*. This was an idea he talked to me about, sitting at the bar of the Formosa Café in Hollywood. Within ten minutes I was committed to doing it. To me, it almost doesn't matter what Tim wants to film – I'll do it, I'm there. Because I trust him implicitly – his vision, his taste, his sense of humour, his heart and his brain. He is, to me, a true genius and I wouldn't use that word with too many people, believe me. You can't label what he does. It's not magic, because that would imply some sort of trickery. It's not just skill, because that seems like it's learned. What he has is a very special gift that we don't see every day. It's not enough to call him a film-maker. The rare title of 'genius' is a better fit – in not just film, but drawings, photographs, thought, insight and ideas.

When I was asked to write the foreword to this book, I chose to tell it from the perspective of what I honestly felt like at the time he rescued me: a loser, an outcast, just another piece of expendable Hollywood meat.

It's very hard to write about someone you care for and respect on such a high level of friendship. It's equally difficult to explain the working relationship betweeen actor and director. I can only say that, for me, Tim need do nothing more than say a few disconnected words, tilt his head, squint his eyes or look at me a certain way and I know exactly what he wants from the scene. And I have always done my best to deliver that to him. So, for me to say what I feel about Tim, it would have to be on paper, because if I said it to his face he would most probably cackle like a banshee and then punch me in the eye.

He is an artist, a genius, an oddball, an insane, brilliant, brave, hysterically funny, loyal, nonconformist, honest friend. I owe him a tremendous debt and respect him more than I could ever express on paper. He is him and that is all. And he is, without a doubt, the finest Sammy Davis Jr impersonator on the planet.

I have never seen someone so obviously out of place fit right in. *His* way.

Johnny Depp
New York City
September 1994

Tim Burton and Johnny Depp on the set of *Edward Scissorhands*

Tim Burton, Johnny Depp and Sarah Jessica Parker on the set of *Ed Wood*

Introduction

In Hollywood, where film-making is a business ruled by profit and loss columns, and respect and admiration are bestowed upon film-makers by virtue of their films' box-office success, Tim Burton is considered to be a genius blessed with the Midas touch. But while his films have, to date, reaped nearly a billion dollars worldwide, they are as far from being slaves to common-denominator commercialism or audience demographics as Burton himself is to fully embracing the Hollywood mainstream in which he has rather uneasily existed throughout his career.

Burton began as an animator at Disney and has continued to operate within the studio system ever since, though he has remained largely removed from its financial imperatives and corporate mentality. Burton's characters are generally outsiders, misunderstood and misperceived, misfits very often encumbered by some degree of duality. They operate on the fringes of their own particular society, tolerated but pretty much left to their own devices. In many ways Burton embodies that contradiction himself; he is embraced for his successes, but in all other ways Hollywood and he maintain a respectful distance from one another. As a consequence, his work has remained as idiosyncratic, imaginative, delightful, and refreshingly inventive as his first film, the five-minute stop-motion short *Vincent*. And, despite the sometimes enormous budgets and productions entrusted to him, his unique, visionary talents have rarely been diluted by concessions to audience expectations.

Batman and its sequel *Batman Returns* may have been the top money makers of their respective years, but they were both deeply disturbed, deeply psychological tales, full of pent-up frustrations, and characters with major personality disorders – including the eponymous hero himself. 'My movies just sort of ended up being representative of the way I am,' Burton says, 'that's the danger of me making big-budget movies. I just get interested in things that I relate to that don't necessarily have anything to do with anybody else.'

Burton's films are, in many ways, as uniquely personal, if not more so than those of Martin Scorsese, Paul Schrader or even Ingmar Bergman. He is a film-maker whose *modus operandi* is based almost entirely on his innermost feelings. For him to commit to a project, it is necessary for him to connect *emotionally* to the characters – be it the millionaire crime-fighter Bruce Wayne of *Batman*, the razor-fingered innocent of *Edward Scissorhands*, or the delusionally enthusiastic film-maker operating on the fringes of Hollywood in *Ed Wood* – connections that, as he is the first to admit, are sometimes far from obvious. *Edward Scissorhands* began as a cry from the heart, a drawing from his teenage years that expressed the inner torment he felt at being unable to communicate with those around him; while his films are, fundamentally, a reaction to his childhood in suburbia.

Growing up, Burton sought solace in the darkened movie theatre, connecting psychologically to those images that flickered on the big screen, while remaining removed from the world around him. His idol was Vincent Price, to whom he paid tribute in *Vincent*, as well as casting him as the inventor father-figure in *Edward Scissorhands*. As a child Burton's passion was monster movies, but while many of his work's recurrent themes and images appear, on the surface, to be a film director graciously paying homage to those youthful inspirations – films such as James Whale's 1931 *Frankenstein* – the reality is often far removed from the obvious. As Burton says, 'The image isn't always literal, but linked to a feeling.'

Given Burton's visual flair, it is perhaps no surprise that he began life in animation, a medium in which literally anything is possible, in which constraints of imagination, time and place have little meaning. In many ways Burton's movies, up to and including *Ed Wood*, can be seen as animated exercises shot as live-action, since they deal with characters and situations that exist outside the realms of reality. 'People ask me when I'm going to make a film with real people? What's real?'

When Burton joined Disney in the late seventies, the studio was in a state of flux, still attempting to come to terms with the death, twelve years earlier, of its founder and guiding light, Walt Disney. When Disney began production on the first full-length animated feature, *Snow White and the Seven Dwarfs* in 1934, it was considered by many to be the folly that would prove to be his undoing. Many predicted it would be an unmitigated disaster, but its extraordinary success, critically and financially, began a legacy that continued up until his death.

The last film that Walt Disney actively had a hand in making was the classic *The Jungle Book*, though he had briefly been associated with *The Aristocats* during its pre-production. The finished film, however, effectively marked the end of the Disney that Walt knew, and signalled the beginning of the decline in quality of both the company's animated and live-action output, a deterioration from which it had yet to recover when Burton joined. Whereas Disney himself had been willing to experiment, the new regime ossified the company in their efforts to play 'safe'. There had been both artistic and fiscal failures during Disney's lifetime, admittedly, but they had been more than outweighed by the certified classics that the studio had turned out, endearing tales such as *Cinderella*, *Pinocchio* and *Fantasia* (although the latter two performed disappointingly at the time of their release). Not only was the output of the new regime bad, it was expensive and bad, with its nadir arguably *The Black Cauldron*, a film to which Burton contributed at the conceptual stage.

Following Walt's death, his brother Roy had assumed control of the company, but he had always been the financial half of the partnership, and his dead sibling's spirit hung for many years like the proverbial albatross round the company's neck. According to those who worked for Disney at that time, decisions were commonly filtered through an unofficial 'what-would-Walt-have-thought?' procedure that continued until 1984 when Walt's nephew, Roy E. Disney, who had resigned as vice-president of the studio seven years earlier, citing creative differences with the then head of Walt Disney Productions Card Walker and head of production Ron Miller, wrestled back control of the company. Roy E. brought in Frank Wells, former vice-president of Warner Bros, and Michael Eisner, former Paramount Pictures president, to head the Walt Disney Studio, and Eisner, together with Jeffrey Katzenberg, his colleague at Paramount, successfully revamped the studio's operations and finally, with *The Little Mermaid* (1989) re-established the company's fortunes as leader in the field of animation, a position it has retained thanks to the success of *Beauty and the Beast*, *Aladdin* and *The Lion King*.

Burton arrived at the studio during a period of intense corporate infighting in the upper echelons of the Disney management and soon found himself stifled creatively by the production-line mentality that was in operation within the company's animation department. Rather bizarrely, and without any precedent, he eventually found himself directing a couple of quirky, black and white shorts, both funded by the studio, one animated (*Vincent*), the other live-action (*Frankenweenie*), which were as highly personal as they were stylish. Neither received much of a release outside the festival circuit, and under different circumstances Burton might very well have remained a conceptual artist, but *Frankenweenie* had its fans and it wasn't long before Burton was on his way.

His first feature, *Pee-Wee's Big Adventure* (1985), was, in hindsight, the perfect outlet for Burton's weirdly wonderful visual manner and particular obsessions – Godzilla movies, stop-motion animation, toys and gadgets. The story of an outsider, Pee-Wee Herman, played by actor Paul Reubens, searching for his stolen bicycle, the film, with alienation a major theme, was at times almost surrealistic in its approach – witness Pee-Wee dancing in stacked heels to 'Tequila' in a biker bar – and also marked the beginning a partnership between its director and composer (Danny Elfman) that has proved to be one of the most creative and fruitful of recent times. An unexpected success, it was three years, however, before Burton directed his next movie, *Beetlejuice* (1988), a supernatural comedy that was a *tour de force* of imaginative design and *outré* special effects. With Michael Keaton as the eminently disgusting bio-exorcist of the title, lead characters who died ten minutes into the film and a storyline that made little to no sense, it was hardly standard Hollywood fare, but managed the difficult trick of being both amusingly gruesome and hysterically funny at the same time. Not all of it worked, but when it did, it was, quite simply, pure genius. Moreover, the film did terrific, if largely unexpected, business, and Burton found himself at the helm of Warner Bros' blockbuster-in-waiting, *Batman* (1989), a film which had been in development at the studio for almost a decade.

Ironically, Burton was never a big comic book fan, but he dug within himself for the necessary emotional connection, delving deep into the Dark Knight's mythology and playing up the character's disturbed, alienated, split-personality, to produce a film that was flawed but which was never less than interesting. Criticized initially for the casting of *Beetlejuice* star Keaton as the film's comic book hero, Burton soon found himself under fire for his movie's brooding, ominous tone and narrative incoherence (the latter accepted by Burton as a given of his directing a movie). But the film, which in Jack Nicholson's show-stealing Joker produced one of the screen's all-time great villains, did phenomenal business, repaying Warner Bros' faith in the youthful Burton tenfold; in addition *Batman* became an unassailable merchandising juggernaut that seemingly consumed the world in its wake. It remains, ultimately, the least satisfactory of all of Burton's work, but its box-office success gave him the freedom to do what he liked.

Edward Scissorhands (1990) remains Burton's most profoundly personal and autobiographical feature. Scripted by novelist Caroline Thompson from Burton's story, it was a fantastical Christmas fairy tale with an amusingly off-centre sense of production design and a strong emotional core, owing in large part to the affecting performances of Burton's cast (Winona Ryder, Dianne Wiest) and in particular to that of

Johnny Depp as the scissor-handed Edward, another of Burton's archetypal outsider figures. In Depp, Burton found an actor who connected with the character's plight in a way that truly transcended the material, and the result was one of the most original, heart-felt and legitimately moving experiences of recent years.

When Burton returned to the world of Batman with *Batman Returns* (1992), he had assumed producing chores from the original team of Jon Peters and Peter Guber and consequently took the film off into far more interesting, if potentially dangerous territories, thanks to a script by Daniel Waters, writer of the venomous high school comedy *Heathers*, which played up the psychological aspects of a cast of comic book characters that included two new villains, The Penguin and Catwoman. The resulting movie, however, failed to deliver the box-office response the studio wanted and expected. Invariably catergorized (and criticized) as too dark, the film did produce a remarkable set of performances in Michael Keaton's haunted Batman and Michelle Pfeiffer's ambiguously schizophrenic Catwoman.

The Nightmare Before Christmas (1993) was a stop-motion musical extravaganza that Burton initially conceived while still working at Disney and which he finally steered through to completion under the direction of fellow Disney alumnus Henry Selick more than a decade later. A tale of misperception, isolation and longing, *Nightmare's* lead character, Jack Skellington, was another of Burton's archetypal outsider figures, embraced by society but existing mainly on its fringes while searching for his own inner happiness.

Burton's latest, *Ed Wood*, represents, on the surface, a departure for the director, dealing as it does with real people and real situations, but again appearances can be deceptive, since this biopic of Edward D. Wood Jr relates the story of yet another outsider – a film-maker and transvestite who existed on the fringes of Hollywood society – whose relationship with his great childhood idol, Bela Lugosi, can be said to mirror in some ways Burton's own relationship with his idol Vincent Price. While discussing Wood, Burton mused that the line between success and failure, talent and the lack of it, is a very thin one, drawing comparisons between Wood and himself that go far beyond the emotional and into the territory marked artistic. There is, it must be stressed, no comparison. Wood was a man whose dreams outweighed his own reality. Burton is a film-maker whose dreams have touched all our realities.

Mark Salisbury
1994

Childhood in Burbank – Cal Arts

Tim Burton was born on 25 August 1958 in Burbank, California, the first son of Bill and Jean Burton. His father worked for the Burbank Parks and Recreation Department, while his mother ran a gift shop called Cats Plus in which all the merchandise featured a feline motif. They had one other child, Daniel, who is three years younger and works as an artist. The Burtons' house was situated directly under the flight path of Burbank Airport and Tim would often lie in the garden, gaze up at the planes flying overhead and time the exhaust fumes floating down from them. Between the ages of twelve and sixteen, he moved in with his grandmother, who also lived in Burbank, and then later into a small apartment above a garage which she owned, paying the rent by working in a restaurant after school. Situated within the Los Angeles city limits, Burbank was then, as it is now, an outpost of Hollywood. Warner Bros, Disney, Columbia and NBC all have their studios there, but in every other way Burbank is an archetypal working-class American surburb. It was an environment, however, from which Tim Burton felt alienated at an early age, one that he would later portray in Edward Scissorhands. *Indeed, it's easy to see the young, introverted Tim Burton in Edward's stranger-in-a-strange-land, removed from his hilltop castle home to a pastel-coloured version of suburbia. As a child, Burton was, by his own admission, moderately destructive. He would rip the heads off his toy soldiers and terrorize the kid next door by convincing him that aliens had landed. He would seek refuge from his surroundings in the movie theatre or sit in front of the television watching horror movies.*

If you weren't from Burbank you'd think it was the movie capital of the world with all the studios around there, but it was and still is very suburban. It's funny, the areas around Burbank have gotten less suburban, but somehow Burbank still remains the same. I don't know how or why, but it has this weird shield around it. It could be Anywhere USA.

As a child I was very introverted. I like to think I didn't feel like anybody different. I did what any kid likes to do: go to the movies, play, draw. It's not unusual. What's more unusual is to keep wanting to do those things as you go on through life. I think I was the quiet one at school. I don't have a real perception of myself. I don't really remember. I kind of floated through things. I didn't consider them the best years of my life. I didn't cry at the prom. I didn't think it was going to be all downhill. I *had* friends. I never really fell out with people, but I didn't really retain friends. I get the feeling people just got this urge to want to leave me alone for some reason, I don't know why exactly. It was as if I was exuding some sort of aura that said 'Leave Me The Fuck Alone'. For a while I looked like I could have been on a casting call for *The Brady Bunch*: I had bell-bottom pants and a brown leisure suit. But punk music was good, that helped me, it was good for me emotionally. I didn't have a lot of friends, but there's enough weird movies out there so you can go a long time without friends and see something new every day that kind of speaks to you.

There were five or six movie theatres in Burbank, but systematically they got taken away. And so for a few years when I was a teenager, there weren't any. But there used to be ones where you could see these weird triple bills like *Scream Blackula Scream*, *Dr Jekyll And Sister Hyde* and *Destroy All Monsters*. Those were the good days of cinema, those great triple bills. And I would go to the cinema on my own, or with a couple of kids in the neighbourhood, whatever.

Recently I went back to Catalina Island. I hadn't been there since I was a kid. I used to go there a lot, and there is this really cool theatre there, The Avalon, and it was done out in these incredible art deco shells. I remember seeing *Jason and the Argonauts* there. I remember both the theatre and the movie, because they seemed to be as one, the design of the theatre, that movie, and the kind of mythology it evoked. It was incredible. That was one of the first movies I remember. It was sometime early, somewhere before I was fifteen.

There was also a period in time when they'd show movies on television on Saturday afternoons, movies like *The Brain that Wouldn't Die*, where the guy gets his arm ripped off and rubs his bloody stump along the wall before he dies, while a head on a plate starts laughing at him. They wouldn't show that on TV now.

I've always loved monsters and monster movies. I was never terrified of them, I just loved them from as early as I can remember. My parents said I was never scared, I'd just watch anything. And that kind of stuff has stuck with me. *King Kong, Frankenstein, Godzilla,* the *Creature from the Black Lagoon* – they're all pretty much the same, they just have different

Fighting Ray Harryhausen's skeletons in *Jason and the Argonauts*

rubber suits or make-up. But there was something about that identification. Every kid responds to some image, some fairy-tale image, and I felt most monsters were basically misperceived, they usually had much more heartfelt souls than the human characters around them.

Because I never read, my fairy tales were probably those monster movies. To me they're fairly similar. I mean, fairy tales are extremely violent and extremely symbolic and disturbing, probably even more so than *Frankenstein* and stuff like that, which are kind of mythic and perceived as fairy-tale like. But fairy tales, like the Grimms' fairy tales, are probably closer to movies like *The Brain that Wouldn't Die*, much rougher, harsher, full of bizarre symbolism. Growing up, I guess it was a reaction against a very puritanical, bureaucratic, fifties nuclear family environment – me resisting seeing things laid out, seeing things exactly as they were. That's why I think I've always liked the idea of fairy tales or folk tales, because they're symbolic of something else. There's a foundation to them, but there's more besides, they're open to interpretation. I always liked that, seeing things and just having your own idea about them. So I think I didn't like fairy tales *specifically*. I liked the *idea* of them more.

For a while I wanted to be the actor who played *Godzilla*. I enjoyed those movies and the idea of venting anger on such a grand scale. Because I was quiet, because I was not demonstrative in any way, those films were my form of release. I think I was pretty much against society from the very beginning. I don't know any children, I don't have any children and I don't like the phrase 'remaining like a child', because I think it's kind of retarded. But at what point do you form ideas and at what point are you shaped? I think these impulses to destroy society were formed very early.

I went to see almost any monster movie, but it was the films of Vincent Price that spoke to me specifically for some reason. Growing up in suburbia, in an atmosphere that was perceived as nice and normal (but which I had other feelings about), those movies were a way to certain feelings, and I related them to the place I was growing up in. I think that's why I responded so much to Edgar Allan Poe. I remember when I was younger, I had these two windows in my room, nice windows that looked out on to the lawn, and for some reason my parents walled them up and gave me this little slit window that I had to climb up on a desk to see out of. To this day I've never asked them why; I should ask them. So I likened it to that Poe story where the person was walled in and buried alive. Those were my forms of

Godzilla venting his anger

4

Vincent Price

connection to the world around me. It's a mysterious place, Burbank.

Vincent Price was somebody I could identify with. When you're younger things look bigger, you find your own mythology, you find what psychologically connects to you. And those movies, just the poetry of them, and this larger-than-life character who goes through a lot of torment – mostly imagined – just spoke to me in the way Gary Cooper or John Wayne might have to somebody else.

Together with a group of friends I would make Super 8 movies. There was one we made called *The Island of Doctor Agor*. We made a wolfman movie, and a mad doctor movie, and a little stop-motion film using model cavemen. It was really bad and it shows you how little you know about animation at the beginning. These cavemen had removable legs – one was in the standing position, and the other was in a walking one – and we just changed the legs. It's the jerkiest animation you'll ever see. I used to love all those Ray Harryhausen movies – *Jason and the Argonauts*, *The Seventh Voyage of Sinbad* – they were incredible, I loved stop-motion animation as a kid. And as you get older, you realize that there's an artistry there too, and that's what you're responding to.

I got through school, but I wasn't interested in the curriculum. I'm of that unfortunate generation that grew up watching television rather than reading. I didn't like to read. I still don't. So what better way to get a good grade than to make a little movie? I remember one time we had to read a book and do a twenty-page book report, but I decided to do a movie called *Houdini* instead. I shot myself on black and white Super 8, speeded up. It had me escaping from the railroad tracks and then being dumped in a pool and escaping again – all these stupid Houdini tricks. It was really fun to do. I didn't read any book, it was just me jumping around in my backyard. It was an easy way to get an A, and I certainly got a higher grade than if I had attempted to talk my way through a written report. That was in early junior high. I must have been about thirteen. And then I did one on psychology for high school. I just took a lot of pictures of books and played them to Alice Cooper's 'Welcome To My Nightmare'; deeply psychological. And I shot a bean bag chair in stop-motion attacking me in my sleep. That was the ending, I think.

I never actually thought about making films for a living. Maybe somewhere deep inside, but I never consciously said I wanted to be a filmmaker. I liked doing it. It helped me get through school. Before Universal Studios became what it is now, they used to have a tour which was very low key and I remember being young and going to see the streets where they shot *Dracula* and *Frankenstein*. It was a powerful feeling, and I think that enhanced the romantic aspects of it. I never consciously thought of making films; it's something I lucked into after a couple of years at Disney. Maybe I was just protecting myself, because I don't like to make proclamations. I prefer to be a bit more stream-of-consciousness about things.

While he showed no particular aptitude for schooling, Burton's artistic potential soon began to reveal itself. In the ninth grade he won ten dollars and first prize in a community competition to design an anti-litter poster which adorned the side of garbage trucks in Burbank for two months. At Christmas and Hallowe'en he would earn extra money by painting and decorating Burbank residents' windows with either snowscapes or jack-o'-lanterns, spiders and skeletons, depending on the season.

In some ways I'm all over the place. I can get hyper and kind of unfocused about things. But there are things that help focus you, and make you feel good. If I'm doing a drawing I can become focused, and, in a funny way, it's a calming experience. And that's something I've never forgotten. I like to draw very much, and as a kid that's all you do in class all day. It's great. If you go to a kindergarten class all the children draw the same, no one's better than another. But something happens when you get older. Society beats things out of you. I remember going through art school, and you've got to take life drawing, and it was a real struggle. Instead of encouraging you to express yourself and draw like you did when you were a child, they start going by the rules of society. They say, 'No. No. You *can't* draw like this. You have to draw like *this*.' And I remember one day I was so frustrated – because I love drawing, but actually I'm not that good at it. But one day something clicked in my brain. I was sitting sketching and I thought, 'Fuck it, I don't care if I can draw or not. I like doing it.' And I swear to God, from one second to the next I had a freedom which I hadn't had before. From that point on, I didn't care if I couldn't make the human form look like the human form. I didn't care if people liked it. There was this almost like drug-induced sense of freedom. And I fight that every day, someone saying, 'You can't do that. This doesn't make any sense.' Every day it's a struggle. It's just a question of trying to maintain a certain amount of freedom.

In 1976, when Burton was eighteen, he won a scholarship to attend the California Institute of the Arts (Cal Arts), a college in Valencia, California founded by Walt Disney, with a programme that had been set up the previous year by the Disney Studio as a training school for prospective animators.

In high school I had a teacher who was encouraging, and I got a scholarship to Cal Arts. At Cal Arts we would make Super 8 movies: we made a Mexican monster movie and a surf movie, just for fun. But animation – I thought that might be a way to make a living. Disney basically had had the same animators since *Snow White* and they had taken a very leisurely approach to training new people. I joined the second year of the Disney-funded programme; they were trying to teach all these eager young new recruits to be animators. It was like being in the Army; I've never been in the Army, but the Disney programme is probably about as close as I'll ever get. You're taught by Disney people, you're taught the Disney philosophy. It was kind of a funny atmosphere, but it was the first time I had been with a group of people with similar interests. They were similar outcast types, people who were ridiculed for their liking of *Star Trek* or whatever.

7

You had access to Disney propaganda material. So, if you wanted to see the way Snow White was drawn, you could see the lines under the dress. You were taught by Disney artists, animators, layout people; you were taught the Disney way. At the time there wasn't the diversity in animation that exists now, so Disney, even as low as it was, was a very romantic ideal, and I would say 90 per cent of the class had aspirations to work there.

At the end of the year, everybody would do a little piece of animation and the Disney review board would come out to view them. It was like a draft. They would review all the films, and they would take people to work at the studio from any class, freshman, on up to the final year, with special consideration for those at the end. But they didn't care. If somebody showed particular promise, then they would get picked. So there was always a lot of competition and speculation about who was going to get picked. It was very intense, and there were always a few surprises each year. I was there three years. I don't know if I would have gone there a fourth, because during the last year I spent almost every day in the financial aid office, because they gave me a scholarship and then they took it away; it was an expensive school, and I could only afford it with that scholarship. As the years went on, the competition, the films, would get more elaborate, there was sound, music, even though they were basically pencil tests. The last one I did was called *Stalk of the Celery Monster*. It was stupid, but I got picked. It was a lean year, and I was lucky, actually, because they really wanted people.

Disney and *Vincent*

Burton joined Disney in 1979 and went to work as an animator on the studio's The Fox and the Hound.

Disney and I were a bad mix. For a year I was probably more depressed than I have ever been in my life. I worked for a great animator, Glenn Kean. He was nice, he was good to me, he's a really strong animator and he helped me. But he also kind of tortured me because I got all the cute fox scenes to draw, and I couldn't draw all those four-legged Disney foxes. I just couldn't do it. I couldn't even fake the Disney style. Mine looked like road kills. So luckily I got a lot of far-away shots to do. But it was not good; it was like Chinese water torture. Perhaps it was just the film I was working on. Imagine drawing a cute fox with Sandy Duncan's voice for three years. It's not something that you can relate to very much. I didn't

The Fox and the Hound

9

have the patience for it, I couldn't do it – which was probably a good thing.

But what's odd about Disney is that they want you to be an artist, but at the same time they want you to be a zombie factory worker and have no personality. It takes a very special person to make those two sides of your brain coexist. So I was very emotionally agitated at that time and couldn't really function very well. I learned how to sleep sitting up with a pencil in my hand. It was so bad. For a while I would sleep a good eight to ten hours a night, and then I would go to work and sleep a good two hours in the morning, and then two hours in the afternoon, sitting up straight, so if anybody walked in I had my pencil at the ready.

I was very strange back then. I could see I had problems. I was always perceived as weird. I would sit in a closet a lot of the time and not come out, or I would sit up on top of my desk, or under my desk, or do weird things like get my wisdom teeth out and bleed all over the hallways. But I've gotten over that. I don't sit in a closet any more. I was kept at arm's length, but at the same time they let me be. I guess I did enough work not to get fired. I just had to do it fast, and because I couldn't draw it anyway, it didn't matter how much time I spent on it. It was probably better if I didn't spend too much time on it. I was weird at that stage. I was having emotional problems. I didn't know who I was.

But because I did these other kinds of drawings, people would see them and I got to do other things. The company was in a kind of screwy stage at that time. They were making things like *Herbie Goes to Monte Carlo*; nobody knew what was going on there. It was like a hermetically sealed world, and I got to move around a little bit in this weird sort of 'non-structure' structure. I got to try different things, to do concepts for live-action and animated projects.

There used to be this guy at Disney in the early days who was paid to come up with ideas and just do drawings. The animators liked his stuff, and he would draw whatever he wanted, like a hand with an eyeball on it. And I worked myself into that kind of position, as a sort of conceptual artist, which was really great. Then it started to turn fun again because I got to do whatever I liked, just sniff magic markers all day.

I was hired as a conceptual artist on *The Black Cauldron*, which was great because for several months I just got to sit in a room and draw any creature I wanted to: witches, furniture, just things. But then, as the film started to get closer to being a reality, they put me with this guy, Andreas Deja, who's a good strong animator in the old, character-driven style, a style completely different from mine. They said to me, 'Tim, we like your

The Black Cauldron

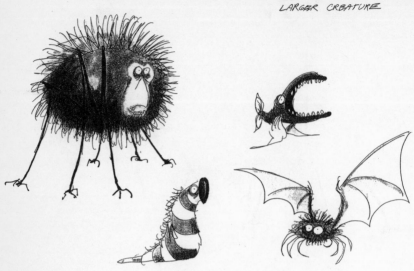

WHEN ANIMALS ARE FRIGHTENED THEY JOIN TOGETHER TO FORM A LARGER CREATURE

The elements …

ideas, but Andreas is more what we want.' I guess they wanted us to mate and have offspring of some kind. He would sit on one side of the room and I would sit on the other. It was like a friendly version of *The Odd Couple*.

So he ended up doing his thing and I did mine. I didn't see the movie, but they didn't use one single concept of mine. I basically exhausted all of my creative ideas for about ten years during that period. And when none of it was used, it was kind of funny. I felt like a trapped princess. I had a great life, in a way. I was able to draw anything I wanted, but it was like working in this completely sealed environment in which you would never see the light of day. But there was always something that made it worthwhile, like doing the *Vincent* short and then the *Frankenweenie* one. Those things were unheard of. So I was lucky enough that everything led to a little higher level.

I did some conceptual work over ten years ago on that Barry Levinson movie *Toys*. I don't think he even knows that I worked on it, but the guy at Disney asked me to do some conceptual stuff. There were still the remnants from the old days at Disney, there were still people who would say, 'Let's do another *Fantasia*', guys from the old school where they didn't

… joined together

have scripts, just a couple of zany gag men in a room who'd say, 'Let's get Louie Prima in here and work up a little number.' Those guys were still around. It was cool.

I remember when they were doing that movie *Tron*. I was just a lowly in-betweener at the time, and there were all these computer guys pitching stuff that only now they are able to do, and not even all of it. It seemed like a company in puberty really, that awkward stage where you're still stuck in the past. I remember when I first got to Disney they were still talking about Walt and it was like this weird mantra: 'Walt would have done this.' And it was like, 'How do you know?' Then, it seemed to me, they realized they needed to come into the twenty-first century but they didn't quite know how to do that. The movies that they made then were awkward. My impression was of a company being run by people who were the third or fourth on the tier – when the talented people left, retired or died they were left in charge.

While working as a conceptual artist, Burton found himself two allies in the shape of Disney executive, Julie Hickson, and Head of Creative

13

Trick or Treat

Trick or Treat

Development, Tom Wilhite, who had begun to see in his drawings a rather unique talent that while not typically Disney was one they felt deserved to be nurtured. And so in 1982 Wilhite gave Burton $60,000 to *produce* Vincent, *a stop-motion animated short based on a poem Burton had written in verse in the style of his favourite children's author Dr Seuss.*

I had been working there about a year to a year and a half, maybe two years – I'm not very good with time. But by that stage I had worked on *The Black Cauldron*, I had worked on a thing called *Trick or Treat* for which I don't think there was even a script, just a concept: a haunted house, kids, Hallowe'en. I had written this *Vincent* story, and I was bored, I was about ready to walk. I couldn't take it any more. But there were a few people there who were very supportive of me, and they gave me a little money to do *Vincent* under the guise of it being a stop-motion test. It was very very nice of them to do that, and that kept me going for a while.

I had written *Vincent* originally as a children's book and was going to do it that way first. But then I got the opportunity to make it as a stop-motion film. I wanted to do that kind of animation because I felt there was a gravity to those three-dimensional figures that was more real for that story. That was really important to me, I wanted it to feel more real.

Together with fellow Disney animator Rick Heinrichs, stop-motion animator Steven Chiodo and cameraman Victor Abdalov, Burton toiled away for two months and came up with the five-minute film. Shot in stark black and white in the style of the German expressionist movies of the 1920s, Vincent *relates the story of seven-year-old Vincent Malloy, a somewhat disturbed child who fantasizes that he is Vincent Price. Flitting between the reality of his banal suburban existence and his fantasy world,* Vincent *imagines himself in a series of situations inspired by the Vincent Price/Edgar Allan Poe films that had had such an affect on Burton as a child, including experimenting on his dog – a theme that would subsequently reappear in Burton's next project* Frankenweenie – *and welcoming his aunt to his home while simultaneously conjuring up the image of her dipped in hot wax. The film ends with Vincent lying on the ground in the dark quoting Poe's 'The Raven'.*

Vincent Price, Edgar Allan Poe, those monster movies, those *spoke* to me. You see somebody going through that anguish and that torture – things you identify with – and it acts as a kind of therapy, a release. You make a connection with it. That's what the *Vincent* thing really was for me. The

'The Raven'

film just goes in and out of Vincent's own reality. He identifies and believes that he's Vincent Price, and you see the world through his eyes. It clicks in and out of reality so to speak, and it ends with a quote from 'The Raven'. The people at Disney thought he died, but he's just lying there. Who's to say whether he's really dead or beautiful in his own little dream world? They wanted it to have more of an upbeat ending, but I never saw it as being downbeat in any way. It's funny, I think it's more uplifting if things are left to your imagination. I always saw those tacked-on happy endings as psychotic in a way. They wanted me to have the light click on and have his dad come in and go, 'Let's go to a football game or a baseball game.' That was my first encounter with the happy ending syndrome.

I never directly linked the shots in *Vincent* to any specific films. There are no real shots from those Poe movies per se. It's just more a matter of growing up and loving those movies than it is direct linkage in terms of shots. There's a *House of Wax* thing, there's some burying alive, some experiments, but I was more concerned with trying to get the stop-motion to work.

House of Wax

Anyone who has seen Vincent *can be in no doubt that the title character, a pasty-faced youth with black, straggly hair, bears a striking resemblance to his creator.*

Well, I never consciously go, 'I'm going to do a drawing that looks like me', but yeah, it's certainly based on feelings that I had, for sure. But anything, even things that are perceived as commercial, like *Batman*, anything that people would find no personal, redeeming qualities in, for me, I've got to be in it to some degree. Even if it's just a feeling. You invest so much in it, there has to be something you identify strongly with. And *Vincent* is certainly more pointedly specific to the way I felt. People would say, 'That's you Tim', but what am I supposed to say? I don't like to think about that. I like to think about it in terms of a concept. I'm very wary of analysing it too intellectually. I find it gets in the way of the more spontaneous, which I prefer to be if I can. If I start to think too much about it, it's not good. But *Vincent*'s one that I feel really good about letting speak for itself, because it's just what it is. It's very hard in

Hollywood because people like things literal. They don't like it when you leave things open for interpretation, but I like that very much.

The film's expressionistic set design and photography seems reminiscent of Robert Wiene's The Cabinet of Dr Caligari.

I certainly saw pictures of it, in any monster book there were pictures of it. But I didn't see it until fairly recently. I think it probably has more to do with being inspired by Dr Seuss. It just happens to be shot in black and white, and there's a Vincent Price/Gothic kind of thing that makes it feel that way. I grew up loving Dr Seuss. The rhythm of his stuff spoke to me very clearly. Dr Seuss's books were perfect: right number of words, the right rhythm, great subversive stories. He was incredible, he was the greatest, definitely. He probably saved a bunch of kids who nobody will ever know about.

Vincent

SO THEN HE AND HIS HORRIBLE ZOMBIE DOG, COULD GO SEARCHING FOR VICTIMS IN THE DENSE LONDON FOG.

WHERE HE'D BE LEFT TO REFLECT ON THE HORRORS HE'S INVENTED,

Vincent

20

Vincent

21

Vincent

22

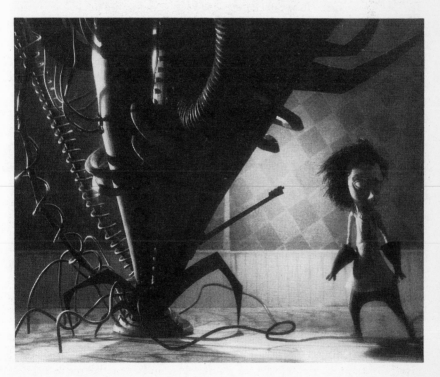

Vincent

Vincent *was narrated by Burton's childhood idol Vincent Price and marked the beginning of a friendship between the director and the actor that lasted until Price's death in 1993.*

We sent Vincent Price the storyboards and asked him to do the narration, and he was incredible. It was probably one of the most shaping experiences of my life. Who knows what it's going to be like? You grow up having a feeling about someone, then you meet them, and what if the guy goes, 'Get the the fuck out of here. Get away from me, kid.' But he was so wonderful, and so interesting as a person in what he liked in terms of art and stuff. He was very supportive. I always had the feeling he understood exactly what the film was about, even more than I did; he understood that it wasn't just a simple homage, like 'Gee Mr Price, I'm your biggest fan.' He understood the psychology of it, and that amazed me and made me feel very good, made me feel that someone saw me for what I was, and accepted me on that level.

It's a scary proposition meeting somebody who helped you through childhood, who had that affect on you, especially when you're sending them something that's showing that impact in a kind of cheesy, children's book kind of way. But he was so great. Those kinds of things are very important to keep you going, emotionally, especially when you run into so many shady characters. Some people are just nice, but he seemed to truly get it. Again, there's a reason why you respond to certain people on the screen – there's some sort of light there, they project something beyond even what their character is.

Vincent *was theatrically released for two weeks in one Los Angeles cinema with the teen drama* Tex, *starring Matt Dillon. But before it was consigned to the Disney vaults, it garnered several critical accolades when it played at festivals in London, Chicago and Seattle, winning two awards at Chicago and the Critics' Prize at the Annecy Film Festival in France.*

Disney were pleased with *Vincent*, but they didn't know what they were going to do with it. It's like, 'Gee, what shall we worry about today, this five-minute animated short film or our $30 million dollar movie?' I felt very happy to have made it. It's cathartic to make anything, to get it done, so that was good, and it got a good response from people who saw it. It was a little odd, though, because Disney seemed to be pleased with it, but at the same time kind of ashamed. I just think they didn't know what to do with it. There's not really a market for a five-minute animated film, and the company was in a strange state of flux, so it didn't rate really high on their priority scale. Plus, I didn't even know whether I was an employee then.

Hansel and Gretel, Frankenweenie and Aladdin's Lamp

Still employed at Disney, Burton next directed a live-action, all-Oriental version of the Grimms' fairy tale Hansel and Gretel *which was produced for $116,000 for the studio's then embryonic cable network The Disney Channel. Written by its executive producer, Julie Hickson, the show lacks* Vincent's *emotional depth, but is a perfect illustration of Burton's outré imagination, deviating from the original Grimms' tale in a variety of uniquely Burtonesque ways, climaxing with a kung-fu fight between Hansel and Gretel and the wicked witch, who is played by a man.*

The Disney Channel had just started and they had a fairy-tale series, and I had this idea of doing *Hansel and Gretel* using only Japanese people and giving it a little bit of a twist. I had a bunch of drawings and they let me do it. Everything, especially early on, was based on drawings. I had a room filled with drawings, and I think that was the thing that made them feel comfortable about me, to some degree. Even though, visually, the drawings aren't easy to imagine in three dimensions, or in any other form than those drawings, I think it made them feel I wasn't completely insane, and that I could actually do something. And again, as a company, they were just kind of floundering around a little bit at that point. Up until very recently, I could never imagine a scenario where I would get to do these things in a studio situation. It was unheard of. I mean now they have those new programmes where studios foot the bill, or they'll invest in film schools. Disney, I think, now tests potential directors by giving them a scene and having them shoot it. But at that time there was no real precedent for what I was doing, and so I was always very aware that the situation I was in was fairly unique. So even when I felt bad, I still felt pretty good.

It follows the fairy tale fairly closely except that it's done with Japanese people. I have always been drawn to the Japanese sense of design. Growing up with *Godzilla* movies, their sense of design and colour really appealed to me, and it has a slight martial arts twist. I liked those martial arts movies, and if you like something, then you like to see it. That was always my attitude. I've never been able to predict or think what an audience would like to see. I've always felt: how can anybody else want to see it if I don't want to? And if I want to see it, and nobody else wants to, then at least I get to see it. So, there's one person who'll enjoy it.

Hansel and Gretel *marked the first time that Burton had worked with actors, albeit a cast of total non-professionals.*

It was pretty amateurish, but that was more to do with me than with them. But I enjoyed doing it, and I learned a lot from it. It's funny, if you've never made a movie with actual people, you think you can do it, you don't see any reason why you can't. It looks very easy. But there is something about it that's abstract. So it was a good learning experience for me. Being an animator, early in my life I rarely spoke to people. I was not a good communicator. I never spoke much – even now – but it used to be worse. I would never finish my sentences; my mind would kind of race

Hansel and Gretel

The witch's house

ahead. It was not like we were doing a Shakespeare play where there was a foundation to it. It was hard to describe to people, and I wasn't very good at it. I think I've got a little better each time I've done it. Obviously, it's a medium where you have to communicate with a large number of people, so that was really the first time I experienced that side of it. I had done it with those Super 8 movies, but this was different, and I think it helped me with the next thing. When I did *Frankenweenie*, I had already learned a lot of stuff from *Hansel and Gretel* in terms of how to deal with people.

Despite its low budget, Burton employed a series of ambitious special effects, including stop-motion animation courtesy of his Vincent *collaborators Heinrichs and Chiodo, as well as a number of on-set visual gags. And by changing Hansel's and Gretel's father's profession from a wood-cutter to a toymaker, Burton indulged in his passion for toys and gadgetry – a trait present in almost all his subsequent work – filling the screen with Japanese 'Transformer' toys.*

Gingerbread
Man

'A weird little puppet who forces Hansel to eat him'

Hansel and Gretel

We had front projection, stop-motion, every FX known to man, but extremely, extremely, extremely crude. It was a great way to try things out. I have always been interested in the combination of live-action and stop-motion animation, stemming from the Harryhausen movies I saw as a kid. This was a very 'designed' kind of thing. It's weirdly ambitious on the one hand, and on the other it's really cheesy and cheap. I don't know where that thing with the toys comes from, however, except that I've always liked toys. I don't recall having an extreme toy fixation or toy fetish. I always saw them as an extension of my imagination – at least that's the way I used them, as a way to explore different ideas. There was a little duck toy that turns into a robot and a gingerbread man. He was a weird little puppet who forces Hansel to eat him.

But there really was no money to make it. I think it showed one night, Hallowe'en, at 10.30 p.m., which for The Disney Channel is like the 4.30 a.m. slot. So, that one didn't go over too big. But there are little moments in it that I like. It was like one of those scary children's shows I grew up watching.

I honestly don't ever recall thinking that I wanted to be a director after I'd made *Hansel and Gretel*. The one thing I did know – and I think I knew this early on, right after the animation experience – was that, whatever I do, it's just got to be more *me*. I can't just pull it together, I'm not proficient enough as an illustrator to fake it. So I didn't say, 'Well, I want to be a director', because that wasn't where my head was. It was more that I was just doing this work, and enjoying it, and I thought the main thing was to create images. It's still true, actually. I think it has less to do with 'I am now a director or a movie maker', and more to do with the joy of creating. And this can be in many forms: images, feelings, *things*, just creating anything.

After that I just kept on developing things, and at that point I was developing *The Nightmare Before Christmas* concept. Often when I was developing something it wasn't a case of 'Now I'm going to develop this', but there would be drawings and the seed of a thought. Things would come out more from a series of sketches. It would be a case of 'This character's kind of interesting', and then discovering what it meant, and uncovering the psychology behind it. Things came about a bit more organically in this period of time. It was not like 'Okay, now I'm doing this, and then I'm going to develop that'; it was much more like a weirdly organic process. It wasn't clean-cut.

Burton's third directorial outing was Frankenweenie, *a stunning twenty-five-minute black and white reworking of James Whale's 1931 version of* Frankenstein *and its 1935 sequel,* The Bride of Frankenstein. *Written by Lenny Ripp from Burton's story,* Frankenweenie *was produced by his champion at Disney, Julie Hickson, and financed by the studio to the tune of almost $1 million. Burton was twenty-five at the time.*

Frankenweenie came out of some drawings and some feelings, and then thinking that maybe this could be good, maybe we could do it as a featurette. I think it was originally intended to go out with *Pinocchio* on its re-release. That whole period of time was very organic. From my thinking of the ideas, to the decision to finance them, none of it could have been planned. When they said yes, I was amazed. I don't think Tom Wilhite was even the head of the department that made the decision to make *Frankenweenie*, it was somebody else. It was odd, none of it made any sense. To this day I'm really bad if people ask, 'How did you become this?' I really have no answer. There's no point A to point B kind of history to it. There's no kind of training that I could look at. It was a completely surreal fluke, the whole thing.

Frankenweenie, *which Burton feels could have been stretched out to feature length if he had been given a few extra days' shooting, updates Mary Shelley's classic story to modern-day suburbia, and follows the adventures of ten-year-old Victor Frankenstein (Barrett Oliver) as he reanimates his pet dog, a bull terrier named Sparky who has been run down and killed in a car accident, in his parents' attic. The film opens with Victor showing his parents a Super 8 movie he's made entitled* Monsters From Long Ago, *featuring Sparky, dressed up as a prehistoric monster and being attacked by a creature straight out of a Godzilla movie. Later, after Sparky has been brought back to life, he is covered in stitching, with a bolt on either side of his neck, a homage to Jack Pierce's make-up for Boris Karloff as the Creature in Whale's* Frankenstein *films.*

You have a dog that you love, and the idea of keeping it alive was the impulse for the film. Again, growing up watching those horror movies, for some reason I was always able to make direct links, emotionally, between that whole Gothic/*Frankenstein*/Edgar Allan Poe thing and growing up in suburbia. *Frankenweenie* was just another outgrowth of that.

But it's very, very important to me, even though there are feelings from *Frankenstein*, that I do not make direct linkage to it. In anything I have ever done, people have always said, 'That's like this sequence in that movie', and it may well be true. But something that's always been very important to me is not to make a direct linkage. If I was to sit down with somebody, and we were to look at a scene from *Frankenstein* and say 'Let's do that', I wouldn't do it, even if it's a homage or an inspired-by kind of thing. In fact, if I ever use a direct link to something, I try to make sure in my own mind that it's not a case of 'Let's copy that'. Instead it's,

Frankenweenie: Victor

33

Frankenweenie: Sparky

'Why do I like that, what's the emotional context in this new format?' That's why I always try to gauge if people get me and are on a similar wavelength. The writer Lenny Ripp was that way. He got it. He didn't want to sit there and go over *Frankenstein*; he knew it well enough. It's more like it's being filtered through some sort of remembrance.

For *Frankenweenie*, I didn't look at anything. I remember thinking the skies in *Frankenstein* were really cool because they were painted. But I didn't go and look at the film because I didn't want to say, 'Do it like that.' I wanted to try to describe it the way I remembered. So I would

Sparky, covered in stitching

describe something, and say, 'It was like a painted backdrop, but the clouds were more pronounced. It was a much more intense, wild sky.' Then when I finally looked at *Frankenstein* I saw that the sky was not quite the way I had described it. That was my impression, but I would still rather go with that. I feel when somebody is just borrowing something, they don't have any feeling for it themselves.

Much like Whale's Frankenstein *(and indeed like* Edward Scissorhands*)*,

Sparky and his bride

Frankenweenie *climaxes with the inevitable showdown between the mob – or in this case, Victor's frightened and angry neighbours – and 'the monster' – Sparky – at a miniature golf course which resembles the setting from Whale's movie. It then culminates in Sparky finding true love in the shape of a poodle whose hairdo resembles that of Elsa Lanchester in* The Bride of Frankenstein. *These references, according to Burton, were again less of a direct link to Whale's films, than a reaction to what he saw around him in Burbank.*

What was great was that you almost didn't even have to think about it, because growing up in suburbia there were these miniature golf courses with windmills which were just like the one in *Frankenstein*. These images just happened to coincide, because that was your life. There were poodles that always reminded you of the bride of Frankenstein with the big hair. All those things were just *there*. That's why it felt so right or easy for me to do – those images were already there in Burbank.

Frankenweenie *marked the first time Burton had worked with a professional cast – which included Shelley Duvall and Daniel Stern as Victor's*

The Bride of Frankenstein

parents, and director Paul Bartel as his teacher – and yet he managed to elicit a number of tender, sympathic performances, from Barrett Oliver, as Victor, in particular.

They were all great. I've been very lucky in that way with actors. I've rarely had experiences where you meet people and it's like the clichéd, horrible, bite-your-head-off kind of thing. It's really shaped my attitude about working with people, actors especially. They need to feel the same about me as I feel about them. If they don't like me, if they're not into me, then I don't want to work with them. All of these people, they knew I had never done anything before, but they liked the idea. They felt that I cared – it's just a little thing, but it's important to me, because there are lots of great actors and you have to connect with them and they need to connect with you. That whole thing of seeking attention, I have never been into that. It's so hard to make something that everybody should be trying to work in the same spirit. And those people were great; everybody was for the project. I think what they did was make me feel comfortable, and I started to learn that you have to communicate with people.

Frankenweenie: Daniel Stern, Shelley Duvall, Barrett Oliver, and Sparky

Frankenweenie *shares with* Vincent *a strong emotive core, a result of their profoundly personal origins. Yet Burton, much like he would later do with* Edward Scissorhands *and* The Nightmare Before Christmas, *passed on the task of writing the screenplay to someone else.*

I never considered myself a writer, even though I do write things. I wrote *Vincent.* Some time I may try it more. But I feel whether or not you write it, you have to feel like you wrote it. I mean, everything I do, I feel like it's me. I guess it was easier and more fun and I could, hopefully, see it a little more clearly by having somebody else write it. I've always felt as long as they get me and get what it is that I feel, then they can bring something to it themselves. Then it's better. It opens it up a little bit more.

Originally intended to be shown with Pinocchio *on its re-release in* 1984, Frankenweenie *was shelved by Disney when it received a PG rating.*

Perception is the one thing that I can't think about, because if I do, it drives me crazy. I can't find logic in how things happen. For instance, it freaked everybody out that *Frankenweenie* got a PG rating, and you can't release a PG film with a G-rated animated film. I was a little shocked, because I don't see what's PG about the film: there's no bad language, there's only one bit of violence, and the violence happens off-camera. So I said to the MPAA, 'What do I need to do to get a G rating?' and they basically said, 'There's nothing you can cut, it's just the tone.' I think it was the fact that it was in black and white that freaked them out. There's nothing bad in the movie. There was a test screening where they showed *Pinocchio* and then *Frankenweenie*. If you ask any child, there are some very intense, scary things in *Pinocchio*. Our perception after not seeing it for a long period of time is that it's a children's classic. It's the same way people feel about fairy tales. When you hear the words 'fairy tale', the first thing that comes to mind is a cute children's story, which is not the way it is. It's the same with *Pinocchio*. It is pretty soft, but there are some intense moments. I remember getting freaked out when I was a kid; I remember kids screaming. And in this test screening kids started crying at certain parts. For kids, it's more horrific than anything in *Frankenweenie*, but because it wasn't a tried and true children's classic with the Good Housekeeping seal of approval, everybody got all freaked out and said, 'We can't release this.'

It was right at the time when the company was changing, when the people who are there now came in. So it met with the same response as *Vincent* in a way, which was 'Oh, this is great, but we have no plans to release it. *Ever*.' I remember being very frustrated because the old regime was out, the new one was in, and again, a thirty-minute short is not a high priority for people who are just coming into a studio and trying to make something of it.

By that point I was really tired of Disney. I felt like 'Okay, this has been really, really great, I'm very, very lucky. Nobody's had the opportunities that I've had. I feel great that I've been able to do this.' But it was a case of doing a bunch of stuff that nobody would ever see. It was kind of weird.

Frankenweenie *did receive a small release in the United Kingdom on a double bill with Touchstone Pictures'* Baby: Secret of the Lost Legend, *and was finally made available on video in the US by Disney prior to the release of* Batman Returns *in 1992. Impressed by his visual style and his dealings with actors, Shelley Duvall invited Burton to direct an episode of Showtime's* Faerie Tale Theatre *series that she hosted and executive-produced. Burton's forty-seven-minute episode,* Aladdin and his Wonderful Lamp, *was his first experience of working with video tape and again featured model and effects work from Rick Heinrichs and Steve Chiodio.*

Right after *Frankenweenie*, Shelley Duvall asked me to do one of the episodes for her *Faerie Tale Theatre*, which was really nice because they basically hired name directors like Francis Coppola and I felt honoured. It was interesting, but it was another case of me being in over my head because it was a tape show with three cameras. Again, some of it is okay and some of it is not. Some of it looks like a bad Las Vegas show. And that's just because when I'm bad, I'm *really* bad. I can't rise above it. I want to keep growing. Everybody wants to stretch. But if I'm not there, if I don't feel right, then I can't fake it too well.

But Shelley created a great atmosphere for that show. She got people there doing it for no money. She was good that way. It was hard work: one week, three cameras; it was intense, and what I realized was that I'm not a very good director-for-hire. I learned that early on. That's why I'm very firm and say, 'Look guys, if you're going to let me do this, then let me do this and I'll try to do the best I can. But it's not going to help to treat me like you might treat a director-for-hire because, you know what, I'll do a really lousy job, and we don't want that.' So I've always tried to protect myself in that sense, and I'm actually in awe of those old directors that could do a Western and then a thriller. It's very admirable, and I'm fascinated by it. I just know I'm not that type.

Aladdin's cast featured James Earl Jones (who provided the voice of Darth Vadar in the Star Wars *trilogy) in two roles, including that of the genie of the lamp, and Leonard Nimoy (*Star Trek's *Mr Spock) as the villainous Moroccan magician intent on possessing the lamp.*

It's surreal to work with those people who you've watched as you grow up, especially when you first get into it. But my first experience with Vincent Price on *Vincent*, that was the ultimate. My mind had been blown once before, so now these were kind of great little explosions. Again, I got a chance to see great actors at work; every actor has a different way of working and so I was observant and learnt from that.

While Aladdin *is reminiscent of* The Cabinet of Dr Caligari *with its skewed set design, it features a number of other images that have, in one form or another, found their way into Burton's subsequent work – bats, skeletons, skulls, spiders and topiaries.*

Once that stuff is inside you, you don't know how long it's going to take to exorcize it. I remember thinking, 'You know what, I've done this. I don't feel this inside me any more. I don't need to see another skeleton.' But then there are times where it's, 'You know what, I just love those skeletons. I thought I was through with them, but I just love them.'

You never know when something is going to be exorcized out of you; those movies are a part of you, part of your make up. That imagery becomes a part of you; it's not even something you think about too much. I try not to think, 'Have I done this before?', because I actually find it's interesting for me to look back and see connections. I haven't really done too much of that, but I do it a little bit. After I did three movies I started to see thematic kinds of things. The process I pretty much go through is: 'Oh, that must mean something to me, deeply.' I find you learn more about yourself if you don't intellectualize right away, if you try to go more intuitively, and then you look back and see what themes and images keep coming up. Then I start to get psychologically interested in discovering what it means, where it's founded. And I find that I learn more about myself. I don't trust my intellect as much, because it's kind of schizy; I feel more grounded going with a feeling.

Pee-Wee's Big Adventure

Having finally left Disney, and with Frankenweenie *receiving good word of mouth within industry circles, it was only a matter of time before Burton secured a feature to direct. What nobody, least of all Burton himself, could have predicted, however, was that the project would be so in tune with his artistic and creative sensibilities. Pee-Wee Herman, aka comedian Paul Reubens, a weirdly asexual, grey-suited personality with a red bow-tie, rouged cheeks and a beloved bicycle, had achieved cult status with his children's TV show* Pee-Wee's Playhouse. *Warner Bros were looking to turn Pee-Wee from TV star to film sensation, and in Burton, who was only 26 at the time, they found the perfect man to do it.*

I was just waiting around, and there was this woman at Warner Bros, Bonnie Lee, she was sort of a friend, and she brought me to the attention of the people over there, and I got the *Pee-Wee* movie fairly easily. That was the easiest job I have ever got, I mean, any job, even a restaurant job, and any movie before or since. Bonnie showed *Frankenweenie* to the Warner Bros people. They showed it to Paul Reubens and the producers of the movie, and it was like, 'Do you want to do this movie?' and I said, 'Yeah.' It was great. It was perfect, because I liked the material, and I felt very comfortable that I would be able to support it because Paul's character was so strong. He *was* Pee-Wee.

I also just liked the fact that he was into his own thing: his bike. In most movies the plot device has to be something that is of importance, and what was of importance to him was his bike.

It's hard for me to imagine a first movie, unless I had created it myself, that I could have related to as well as I did to *Pee-Wee*. It was so easy to realize it because I could feel it very easily. It was all scripted, except for tiny bits here and there. Some of the visual jokes weren't scripted, like when he's in the bathroom and he looks out through the fish tank window. But since the character was so strong it allowed us to focus on certain visual things.

I loved the movie and felt so connected to it because there was a lot of

Pee-Wee's Big Adventure: Paul Reubens and bicycle

imagery that I liked. I could add, but I wasn't imposing my own thing on it completely. I got to take the stuff that was there and *embellish* it. There were a few things that I added, but I was just lucky to be so clearly in synch with Paul. It would have been a real nightmare if I hadn't been in synch with him; I would have been fired because he was the star and it was his movie.

I remember seeing Paul's show and loving it because it really tapped into the permanent adolescence thing, and I completely connected with that. It was good for me too, because at that point in my life I really wasn't the best communicator, and it would have been a nightmare if we hadn't been so in synch. What he liked, for the most part, I liked; what I liked, for the most part, he liked. So we just did it.

'It really tapped into that permanent adolescent thing'

I've always felt close to all the characters in my films. I've always felt I *had* to be, because when you're doing something you're putting your life into it, and there has to be aspects to all the characters that are either a part of you, or something you can relate to, or something that is symbolic of something inside you. I *have* to connect. The Pee-Wee character was just into what he was doing, and when you grow up in a culture where people remain very hidden, it was nice that he didn't really care about how he was perceived. He operated in his own world, and there's something I find very admirable about that. He's a character who is on his own, who is able to operate in society, and yet he's also sort of an outcast. Again, it's that whole theme of being perceived as this weird thing. In some ways, there's a freedom to that, because you're free to live in your own world. But it's a prison in a way. It's how I felt when I was an animator at Disney.

Written by Phil Hartman, Michael Varhol and its star Paul Reubens, Pee-Wee's Big Adventure centres around Herman's quest to retrieve his stolen bike, a search that takes him on a road trip across America, from a dinosaur park in Palm Springs, down to the Alamo and back to Burbank, encountering all manner of American film archetypes, including a biker gang, an escaped prisoner and a waitress out to better herself. It was a journey which allowed Burton to indulge in his penchant for stop-motion animation. Firstly, in a dream sequence in which a Tyrannosaurus rex – animated by regular collaborator Rick Heinrichs – chows down on Pee-Wee's bike, and secondly, in the film's most memorable sequence, when Pee-Wee encounters Large Marge, a ghostly female truck driver whose face distorts in front of his eyes.

There's an energy with stop-motion that you can't even describe. It's to do with giving things life, and I guess that's why I wanted to get into animation originally. To give life to something that doesn't have it is cool, and even more so in three dimensions, because, at least for me, it feels even more real. With the Large Marge thing or the dinosaur – any time we could throw in some stop-motion, the better. We would have had a lot more if they'd have let us.

The movie-making process is weird, because the Large Marge sequence

Transformation: Large Marge

45

The dinosaur dream

was in the script originally, and there was lots of talk about how to do it; we even talked about not having anything, just Paul screaming, and let that be the joke. It's funny, whenever I see the movie with an audience that sequence almost always gets the biggest laugh. You can tell that was the thing that kept people going for the whole movie, it carried people along, and it's so scary because I almost cut out the best thing before an audience saw it. It was a special effect and those are the first things to go.

I completely storyboarded *Vincent*. I storyboarded at least half of *Frankenweenie* and a friend of mine did the rest, while on *Pee-Wee* I got a guy to board it. From movie to movie they've gotten boarded less and less and what I've done since then is little sketches. On *Pee-Wee*, because it was my first film, they wanted to know that I'd got the shot list, that I could make the day. So it was helpful, and I liked that. It was my background, so I felt comfortable. Again, since I wasn't very good at speaking, this visual representation was helpful.

A lot of people in the movie were from improv groups like The Groundlings, and I started to get really into it, because when people are good at improv, it's really fun and it's kind of liberating. And so I started to feel that I was going to storyboard less because it's more fun to build up to a spot and let it happen on the stage. You have to have enough of an idea to know what you're doing, but as much as you plan, there's something about the reality of being on the set with the actors, costumes, lights and the rest of that environment that changes things. Not so much on the *Pee-Wee* movie because that was kind of *there*, but in later movies, it's like 'This line may sound good, but it's being said by a guy in a bat-suit, so I don't know if it's a good line.' You may think it's a good line, but it's not until you get on that stage, at that moment, with these weird characters that it's right. So I loosened that up a lot. On *Beetlejuice* it was even more so because Catherine O'Hara and Michael Keaton are so good at improv.

It started with Paul and one of the writers, Phil Hartman, who is on *Saturday Night Live* now. Those guys were really good and funny, and working on that movie was a lot like being in animation and having a story meeting; even though the script was really good, we'd sit around and come up with ideas. It was very exciting to me to be around them because they were funny. In improv, they base everything on knowing what their character is and letting it go from there. In *Pee-Wee* it was a case of having the elements there already: he's got these bunny slippers and there's a little toy carrot, so you have the slippers go and sniff the carrot. One thing that was completely improvised was that whole thing in the Alamo with the guide. That was the first time that there was a good chunk of improvisation and the girl who did that, Jan Hooks, was really good and ended up on *Saturday Night Live*. All these people from The Groundlings, people from improv, I have a real respect for them because it's the way I like working: it starts with a very good foundation and then kind of goes free.

Pee-Wee's Big Adventure climaxes with a bicycle ride on the Warner Bros backlot. It's almost Felliniesque in content and tone as Pee-Wee Herman, reunited with his beloved red and white bicycle, is pursued through a series of soundstages disrupting the filming taking place on each one. The movies in question reflect Burton's preoccupations and interests: a beach movie, a Christmas number, a Japanese monsterfest with Godzilla – though, he says, the majority of the films were in fact present in the original script.

I think I added a couple. But all those genres were stuff that I liked very much; that monster fighting Godzilla was the Giddra, otherwise known as Monster Zero. Working on the Warner Bros backlot was kind of magical. Shooting on a soundstage *is* magical. That magic has worn off a little since then, unfortunately, because of the business side surrounding Hollywood, the torture aspects of it. I kind of get freaked out when I go to studios now because there's a negative as well as a positive side, whereas before there just used to be a positive one.

While Burton had previously used composers Michael Convertino and David Newman to score Frankenweenie *and* Aladdin, *to provide the music for* Pee-Wee's Big Adventure *he chose Danny Elfman, lead singer with the cult group Oingo Boingo Band, who had never scored a film before.*

Before I was in the movies I'd go see them in clubs. I had always liked their music. Of all the groups that I went to see, which was mainly the punk kind of stuff, which I love, I always felt that because they had more people in the band and used weirder instruments, the music seemed to be more story-oriented in some way, more filmic. So when the *Pee-Wee* movie came about, it was great, because being low-budget they were more willing to take a chance. They took a chance on me, they took a chance on Danny. Their attitude was to surround me with a bunch of old pros, but music was the one area which that didn't carry over into. Hearing the music played by an orchestra was probably one of the most exciting experiences I've ever had. It was incredible and so funny to see Danny because he'd never done anything like that. It's always magical when you've never done something. I guess it's like having sex: it can be great, but it's never quite the same as that first time. Music is always important, but that was really the first time where it was like a *character*, definitely a character.

Danny was great because he had never done this and so it was good for me because I got to go through the process. He got a tape of the film and I would go over to his house, and he'd play little things on his keyboard so I could see it right there. We were definitely on the same wavelength. It was good because what he couldn't verbalize, or what I couldn't verbalize, didn't matter because it was there and he got it. It was pretty much like, 'It's great, it's perfect', and it's so much easier when that's the case. I've always tried to be very sensitive; if you find the right people, you're almost on a different level.

Because it was a low-budget movie it wasn't high on Warner Bros' priorities, but at the same time *The Goonies* was being shot across the way and they had these huge sets, and, I don't know, they may have been on schedule, maybe it was just me who wasn't, but the executives passed by that stage every day and would come down and start yelling at me, 'What are you doing? You're taking all this time?' They were on our case, but it didn't teach me anything, except to have a worse temper and go faster. It's at that stage that you learn that movie-making is not an exact science. The thing that has always bothered me is that nobody was irresponsible. It was like, 'I wish this was going faster', but we were dealing with animals and elements and FX. We weren't doing anything crazy, we weren't overshooting. I even cut stuff out as we were going along because we didn't have time. But we were just a small thing. It's show-business hierachy, in a way. They won't torture A list people, but they'll torture the B list, because they can.

To be a director you can't have any fear. At best, you probably have to have a very healthy balance of not being an egomaniac, but with enough security in yourself to just go for it. Also, I think the unknown helps. Actually, you get more freaked out as you go along and the experiences pile up on you; you find yourself getting weirder. I found that on my first feature, I was the most secure and unfreaked out than at any other time since. I had the greatest time.

I was the worst in school for learning anything. If somebody tells me something, I have some reaction against hearing it, I just will not listen. It's why I'm so bad with names. I don't know where that's from. It probably comes from some weird internal protection. In school I retained *nothing*. All I remember from school are the names of certain clouds. I don't remember dates, I don't remember anything. So I didn't come away from *Pee-Wee* thinking I had learned this or I had learned that, because that experience was probably the purest experience I have ever had, and part of that was me being fairly naïve about the whole situation. I've found that there are a lot of unpleasant things involved in movies and it's best not to dwell on them. It's funny about selective memory because on every movie I've done I've gotten very sick, because I've put a lot of myself into it. I've gotten sick and I've had to keep going and finish the movie, and yet I wanted to die. But those things kind of fade away after a while. It's a good thing. That's why I never like jumping from one movie to another, because it's too much of a harsh experience. Luckily it leaves you, so that you can do it again, but it does get harder and harder.

That's why I think I always liked Fellini movies because he seemed to capture the spirit and the magic of making a movie. It is something that is beautiful and you want to obtain it because it gives you the energy to keep going. But there are a lot of negative sides to it, nothing *really* negative, but it's a harsh experience. The things you learn about movie-making are fine, as you go along you learn about lenses. It's taken me a while, but I gather information each time. You just try to keep learning on a basic technical level. But on the other side, the Hollywood side, there's nothing really to learn that's of any value. A lot of it is not based on logic, and that can be disturbing. If you're trying to find a foundation for something, it's a disturbing thing, so I try not to think too much about it, because I feel more irrational from movie to movie.

Released in the summer of 1985 Pee-Wee's Big Adventure *was a surprise box-office success, though critical opinion was mixed.*

The reviews on Pee-Wee's Big Adventure were *really* bad. I remember one review, and I'll never forget this, which said, 'Everything is great, the costumes are brilliant, the photography is great, the script is fabulous, the actors are all great, the only thing that's terrible is the direction.' One said, 'On a scale of one to ten, ten being best, *Pee-Wee's Big Adventure* gets a minus one.' It's the first minus one I remember seeing. It was on a lot of the ten worst films of the year lists. It's funny, I look at the movie and I don't think it's bad. I love it. There may be some weak passages, but it's really not that bad. It was kind of devasting; I had never really been through that before. There were a couple of good reviews, but for the most part they were pretty bad. Not just on the fence bad, but *bad* bad.

But I think it affected me in a positive way. I've always gotten enough good and bad reviews. I've known people who've gone through that first film thing when they get 'They're the next Orson Welles', and that can kill you. I'm glad I didn't get that. I much prefer the kind of raking over the coals I got because it's a mistake to believe any of it. A lot of the criticism I got was that the film was just images, and I'm thinking, 'It's a movie for Christ's sake, it's not a radio programme, it's a visual thing, so what's wrong?'

Having a background in animation sort of broadens the scope of what you can do visually. Cinema is a visual medium so everything that you do – even if it's not blurting out to the audience on a completely conscious level: 'This is what I am' – everything is meaningful in terms of the look of things. So I always felt having that background in animation was a good tool for me to explore visual ideas and apply them to live action.

The thing I liked about Fellini was that he created images that even if you didn't know what they meant literally, you *felt* something. It's not creating images to create images. And even though I didn't fully understand a lot of what he was saying, I could feel a heart behind it. That's what his work meant to me, that things don't have to be literal, you don't have to understand everything. Even though it may be an extreme image, something that's out of the realm of people's perception of reality, you *feel* something. It's that whole sort of unspoken thing that I find beautiful. That's the magic of movies.

Pee-Wee made money, which was the main thing in Hollywood at that stage of the game. I care about money, which is why I get so intense when these people are on my case saying I don't make commercial movies, because I've always felt very responsible to the people who put up the money. It's not like you're doing a painting. There is a large amount of money involved, even if you're doing a low-budget movie, so I don't want to waste it. In a non-exact science, kind of weird world, you try to do the best you can. I've never taken the attitude of the artiste, who says I don't care about anything, I'm just making *my* movie. I try to be true to myself and do only what I can do, because if I veer from that everybody's in trouble. So I try to maintain that integrity. And when there is a large amount of money involved, I attempt, without pretending to know what audiences are all about, to try and do something that people would like to see, without going too crazy.

You try your best, but it's such a surreal thing. I thought the movie industry was bad, but when you look at other worlds, like fashion or advertising or the art world, it's even more cut-throat and even more full of pretension and bullshit. I think the good thing about the movie industry which protects you from that is that there are so many things that can go wrong, so many elements: the reviews, the box office, and then there's the movie itself. There are so many things that can punch away at you and force you to have a little bit of humility, that it kind of keeps you grounded.

I had a good experience on *Pee-Wee*, I enjoyed it. It was surreal: a lot of the reviews were bad and then the movie did fairly well, which was great. It's hard to imagine a better, more grounding experience in a way because it left me realizing that you've got to just try and hope for the best, maintain some integrity and try to punch through it.

I don't even think they asked me to do the next *Pee-Wee* movie, but it's not something I wanted to do. It was my first movie and I could already see the rut that Hollywood puts people in. You do two *Pee-Wee* movies, and then that's you, which was different for me than it was for Paul. For him that's fine, because that's his character.

Later that same year Burton directed The Jar, *an episode of* Alfred Hitchcock Presents, *a revamped version of the sixties TV series which had been updated by US network NBC and which featured colourised versions of Hitchcock's prologues and epilogues. Scripted by horror novelist Michael McDowell, from Ray Bradbury's original teleplay,* The Jar *starred Griffin Dunne as the owner of the titular container whose misshapen contents have a persuasive effect on those who behold them and featured a score from Danny Elfman and special effects by Rick Heinrichs.*

That was another tough one. I've learned from things like *The Jar* and *Aladdin* that when I get into situations like that it's very dangerous. If I can't do exactly what I want to do – that's not to say that what I want to do is going to work out every time – things just don't work out quite as well. I need that deep connection.

The next year Burton was called in by Brad Bird, who he had worked with on The Fox and the Hound, *to contribute a number of designs to* Family Dog, *an animated episode of Steven Spielberg's television series* Amazing Stories *which Bird was directing, and which was originally part of a showreel the pair had produced during their time at Disney. The episode was subsequently turned into a series by Spielberg's company Amblin for which Burton served as executive producer.*

My involvement was pretty much from a design point of view; I did storyboards and designed some more characters, because I just love the idea of

Family Dog

trying to do something from a dog's point of view. I don't know why, but I always relate to dogs. Edward Scissorhands is like a dog to me.

Beetlejuice

The success of Pee-Wee's Big Adventure *at the American box office meant that Burton was now considered a 'bankable' director. He had begun working on a script for Warner Bros for a proposed* Batman *movie with screenwriter Sam Hamm, but while the studio was willing to pay for the script's development they were less willing to green-light the project. Meanwhile, Burton had begun reading through the scripts that had been sent his way, and was swiftly becoming disheartened by their lack of imagination and originality. That is, until record industry mogul turned film producer David Geffen, whose company had a distribution deal with Warner Bros, handed him a script called* Beetlejuice, *written by Michael McDowell, who had provided the script for* The Jar. *It was, in retrospect, quintessential Burton material: ghoulish, bizarre, highly imaginative with the potential for outrageous set design and innovative special effects. Described by McDowell as 'a feel-good movie about death', it featured Alec Baldwin and Geena Davis as Adam and Barbara Maitland, a happily married New England couple who are killed when their car plunges into the river and who wind up haunting their own home. But when a pretentious New York family – Catherine O'Hara, Jeffrey Jones and Winona Ryder – move in, their quaint spooking techniques prove ineffectual and the Maitlands call in the services of Michael Keaton's bio-exorcist Betelgeuse (pronounced Beetlejuice) to get rid of the intruders.*

I didn't work for a long time between *Pee-Wee's Big Adventure* and *Beetlejuice* because I just didn't want to do the things they were offering me. I was being offered any bad comedy. It was a case of, you do a bad comedy, you get offered *all* the bad comedies. I even got offered *Hot to Trot*, a talking horse movie! Stuff I had passed on before I even started working on *Beetlejuice* had been made and had come out. That's how long a period of time it was.

It was David Geffen who asked me if I wanted to do *Beetlejuice*. I loved it because I had read a lot of scripts that were the classic Hollywood 'cookie-cutter' bad comedy. It was really depressing. Then this script came through the door, and after Hollywood hammering me with the concept of story structure, where the third act doesn't work, and it's got to end with a little comedy, or a little romance, the script for *Beetlejuice* was completely anti all that: it had no real story, it didn't make any sense, it was more like stream of consciousness. That script was probably the most amorphous ever. It changed a lot, but the writer Michael McDowell had a good, perverse sense of humour and darkness, and that was the good thing about it. It had the kind of abstract imagery that I like, with these strange characters and images floating in and out.

We worked on the script for a long time, and some of it came to something, some of it didn't. I wanted to cast Sammy Davis Jr as Betelgeuse, but they nixed that idea. We went through a lot of things; Michael McDowell and (producer) Larry Wilson worked on the script for a while, but they got beaten down by the constant questioning. I mean, for a lot of the time on *Beetlejuice* I felt like I was in court giving depositions. I remember having script meetings that lasted for like twenty-four hours over the course of two days, and by the end of it we were questioning every element of the script which, for me, is not necessarily that productive.

It was time to bring in a fresh fighter, so to speak, in the shape of Warren Skaaren, because Michael and Larry were burnt out. Warren was known at that point as a script doctor, as a sort of straight arrow. And because I was perceived as a crazy kind of loose cannon, I went along with it because I wanted to get it done. If they perceived him as the logical one that was fine with me. So we worked on the script for a long, long time, but the fact of the matter is, a lot of the stuff in the film is improvised, a lot of it was just me going over to Michael Keaton's house and the two of us coming up with jokes. Michael was just so much fun. He would say things like, 'How about some teeth?' and he would put in some teeth and his voice would start to change. It was a building process. It was really fun because we were essentially creating a character. It was the first time I had done that because the Pee-Wee character was *there*. This time I got to be there, watching, creating, being a part of that.

Casting is always a very case-by-case thing for me. It's hard because it's like a puzzle. You go with one person, then you try to find another person, but you don't want to go too much in a certain direction because then it starts looking like TV. Michael Keaton was actually Geffen's idea. I hadn't seen him in anything, which was good, because I don't like seeing people in other things. I prefer to just meet them. I met Michael and that's when I started to see the character of Betelgeuse. I didn't know him that

Beetlejuice: Michael Keaton and Winona Ryder

well, I didn't know his work, but he's crazy. Michael is manic, a livewire, and he's got these great eyes. I love people's eyes, and he's definitely got a wild pair.

I grew up watching Lon Chaney and Boris Karloff. There's a freedom to those performers, even though most people think they're so loaded up with make-up you can't see them, which is an odd thing to me. I've found that when you put make-up on people it actually frees them. They're able to hide behind a mask and therefore show another side of themselves, which is great. What it did for Michael was it allowed him to play somebody who wasn't a human being, and the idea of playing someone who isn't human, behind some cheesy make-up, is very liberating. You don't have to worry about being Michael Keaton, you can be this *thing*. That was very magical to me. And ever since, any time an actor is able to immerse himself behind something, I just love it, because you get to see another side of him. Be it Johnny Depp in *Edward Scissorhands* or Jack Nicholson as The Joker, it's fascinating. It taps into some other side of them. It's like at Hallowe'en, people dress up and it allows them to get a little wilder, they become something else. That's one of the aspects of film-making that I've constantly enjoyed, the transformation of people. For Betelgeuse we wanted Michael to look like he'd crawled out from under a

Sketches for Winona Ryder's character, Lydia

rock, which is why he's got mould and moss on his face.

A lot of the people didn't want to do the movie. The only person who initially really wanted to do it was Geena Davis. The others may have wanted to, but it didn't seem like they did. I understand why, nobody knew what it was, and all I'd ever done was *Pee-Wee's Big Adventure*, and even though it was okay and did fairly well, it was not *Citizen Kane*, I wasn't Preston Sturges, and even the final script is not really about *anything*. But that's what's great about it. We would talk about things that it was about. But it was more like junior high psychology than the Hollywood meaningful-one-sentence kind of pitch. Everybody would read the script, and just go, 'Do I want to do this? I don't know. What is it?' But it was hard to describe because it's the *look*, it's the *feel*, and you can't really describe that until you're in there, doing it. But everybody obviously came on board and was there one hundred per cent. Michael got into it because we talked and he started to think about it in a certain way. But I can see why people weren't lining up to sign on.

Catherine O'Hara was from the SCTV improv troupe which was very popular at the time, and those people were very good at doing characters. I had asked about Winona Ryder because I had seen her in *Lucas* and she had a really strong presence, but I'd heard she didn't want to do it because of the satanic thing. I thought she must be a religious person or something, but then I found out that it wasn't true, because when I met her she wanted to do it and she was great.

Having previously been locked so much into the design ethic predetermined by Paul Reubens's character for Pee-Wee's Big Adventure, Beetlejuice *finally afforded Burton the budget to meld to his unique imagination and hire the artists he wanted to work with, including visual effects supervisor Alan Munro, who initially began storyboarding the film, and production designer Bo Welch, with whom Burton would later collaborate on* Edward Scissorhands *and* Batman Returns.

If you read the *Beetlejuice* script you could imagine it done many different ways, and I think that's what freaked people out. If you're talking about death, you could imagine it in a cruel and horrific way – either that or you could go for the *Heaven Can Wait* approach with clouds and the guy walking along surrounded by fog. With *Beetlejuice*, I had the opportunity to hire a designer who I wanted, and to do more what I wanted to do. I hadn't really seen any of Bo's work, but I just liked him. He cared. It's funny, there are a lot of people who get so freaked out by the movie industry that they just become a part of it, there's no joy in it for them any more, so it's nice to work with people – and this may sound corny – who want to do a good job, who care, and who have an artistic sensibility. It shouldn't be that big a deal, but I guess it is.

I would do a few sketches, then we'd look at things. You start out with a concept, and then build upon that. I always had my own ideas about the way it should be: if there's darkness there should be colour and light. *Beetlejuice* was a real mix of colour and dark to me, and I wanted to temper a lot of the darker aspects and make it a bit more colourful. Again, I never think about it, it's just something I do. It's like, this person would look good with blue skin – it's just a feeling. And you come up with jokes. I would come up with sketches and the effects guy would come up with some sketches. For example, we had this waiting room in the afterlife and I always had it in mind to poke fun at death, and it was a case of thinking what kind of people are we going to put in here? Let's have a guy who's been in a shark attack, a skin diver with a shark on his leg. So, we'd come up with sketches like the magician's assistant who's just been sawn in half, or a guy who's been burnt to death while smoking in bed. We tried to portray the afterlife as a cheap science fiction movie; not as clouds in a beautiful sky, but as an IRS office. I got more of an opportunity to do my thing.

The Waiting Room: poking fun at death

59

Returning behind the camera were cinematographer Thomas Ackerman, who had previously shot Frankenweenie, *and Rick Heinrichs, who was employed as visual effects consultant. Heinrichs, like Burton, had graduated from Cal Arts to a career at Disney, and had been his regular design collaborator ever since* Vincent.

We started out when we were both at Disney. Rick was a sculptor and I had all these weird drawings which nobody believed could be brought into the third dimension. Rick's one of the best sculptors I've ever worked with. He was the only person who I really felt could take an idea, a drawing of mine, and bring it into the third dimension. He wanted to get into the art director end of things. He did some stuff on *Edward Scissorhands*, was art director on *Batman Returns* and visual consultant on *The Nightmare Before Christmas*. But I think it was good for us to do other things. It's like Dean Martin and Jerry Lewis, Rick became so associated with me that it was very important for him to expand his horizons a bit. I think it's been very good for him, and when the time arises we will probably do stuff together again.

The Waiting Room: burned to death smoking in bed

Transformation: Barbara Maitland

Beetlejuice's budget was $13 million with just one million of that given over to special effects work, a paltry sum considering the scale and scope of the effects called for by the script, which included stop-motion, replacement animation, make-up effects, puppetry, blue screen and false perspective. It was always Burton's intention, however, that the special effects be cheap, creaky illusions rather than state-of-the-art effects, a feeling in keeping with the tone of the script, his early work on Hansel and Gretel *and* Pee-Wee's Big Adventure, *and a throw-back to the* Godzilla *movies he loved so much as a child.*

We wanted the effects to be kind of cheesy, and they were. We just tried to be fairly matter-of-fact about it. I didn't want to make too much of a show

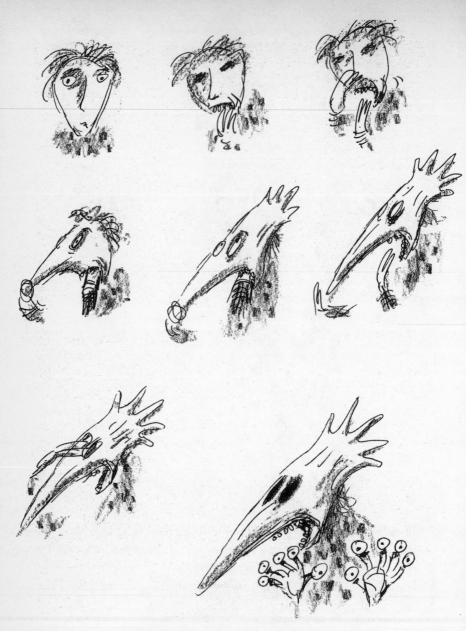

Transformation: Adam Maitland

of it, in a way. Growing up watching the kinds of movies that I did, like Harryhausen, *The Fabulous World of Jules Verne* and *Baron Münchausen*, I always found the effects to be a little more human. There's a certain sort of handmade quality about them, which is probably why I like folk art.

The Maitlands transformed

The handmade feel Burton was after is more than apparent in the sequences in which Geena Davis and Alec Baldwin pull their faces apart and distort their features – effects that are more outré than gruesome.

'We wanted the special effects to be kind of cheesy'

We tried to take the edge off it being gruesome by making them real in their own context. We did a snake in *Beetlejuice* which just didn't work – it looked *too* fake – so I always had my own personal set of standards of what I thought was believable in this world, and what didn't quite make it. It was very much a personal thing.

It worked in *Beetlejuice*, and I continued that philosophy in *Batman*, which was a mistake. It disturbed people. In *Batman* I always loved that whole thing of The Joker pulling out a gun and shooting the Batplane down. But again it's perception. I was doing a giant big-budget movie and people expect a certain kind of thing with that. So while that concept works in *Beetlejuice* and *Pee-Wee*, it doesn't necessarily work when people perceive the movie as a big blockbuster.

Beetlejuice *features a number of visual references that surface continually in Burton's work: these include a model town, characters patterned with black and white stripes, and a graveyard setting.*

There was a graveyard right next to where we lived, about a block away, and I used to play there. I don't know exactly why it keeps showing up, except for the fact that, again, it's part of your soul; it was a place where I felt peaceful, comfortable; a whole world of quiet and peace, and also excitement and drama. It's all those feelings mixed into one. I was obsessed with death, like a lot of children. There were flat tombs, but there was also this weird mausoleum with weird gates on one side. And I would wander around it any time of the day or night. I would sneak into it and play, and look at things, and I always felt really good there.

As for model towns, I used to draw big tableaux of flying saucers attacking an army. They were very elaborate, almost like miniatures in a way. Also when we were shooting those Super 8 movies we used to make miniatures. Again, I don't know why, but all those movies I used to like as a kid had them. It's like stop-motion animation, there's a certain energy and vibe which is quite strong. A lot of it has to do with those *Godzilla* movies.

As far as the black and white stripes are concerned, that one I have never been able to figure out. I guess there must be some sort of prison element involved in there somehow. I *am* drawn to that image, I always have been, it's in a lot of drawings as well, but I don't know why.

Throughout the film Betelgeuse transforms into various guises, the most extreme of which is seen towards the film's climax when Keaton appears wearing a merry-go-round hat, featuring various demonic carousel creatures revolving around its rim, and fifteen-foot-long hammer-weight arms. Designed by Burton and built by special make-up effects artist Robert Short, Keaton's headpiece was topped off with a skull that looks remarkably like Jack Skellington, the main character from The Nightmare Before Christmas.

I would just doodle those things all the time and the images would reoccur in other forms. But I hadn't noticed that until now. I also had bat ears on the thing too and, at the time, I had no idea I was going to be doing *Batman*. Often these images are planted early on, and then later come to be real, which is interesting to me. It shows how the subconscious works.

It was Danny Elfman who again provided the music for Beetlejuice, *creating a fantastical score that was, as with* Pee-Wee's Big Adventure, *as much of a character as Keaton's bio-exorcist. But the soundtrack also featured two calypso songs from Harry Belafonte, including the 'Banana Boat Song', which became the film's unoffical theme tune.*

That was something Warren Skaaren put into the script – the people reacting to a musical number – and he had picked this *Big Chill* yuppie kind of Motown music that was very happening at the time. I didn't want to do it. So I just started listening to a bunch of music, and I liked the Belafonte songs. There was something about Adam and Barbara being on vacation and this kind of calypso music which I liked.

There was a weird incident with *Beetlejuice*. We did some test screenings without the score, and the film got some really low marks. Then we showed it with the score and it got really high marks, and one of the things people liked from these test screenings was the score. But then somebody at the studio said that the score was 'too dark', which was odd because these are the people who live and breathe by these audience research screenings and here they were contradicting the only positive thing from the screening.

The test screenings also suggested to Burton a new coda. Since the response to the afterlife waiting room scenes was so enthusiastic, Burton included an epilogue featuring Betelgeuse foolishly angering a witch doctor, who then sprinkles a powder over Keaton's head causing it to shrink.

Transformation: Betelgeuse

We never really had an ending, so we shot some different things and showed preview audiences a couple; they chose that one. But the movie was so random, in a way, it never really had an ending. It still hasn't, but it's the best we could do.

Beetlejuice *opened in America on April Fool's Day 1988 and was a surprise success, taking $32 million in its first two weeks, eventually grossing more than $73 million. The film won an Oscar for Ve Neill, Steve La Porte and Robert Short for make-up, and seemed to vindicate Burton's theory that audiences could handle films that break with Hollywood conventions. Weird was good, weird was acceptable, weird was successful. Critical reaction too was enthusiastic: Pauline Kael called the movie 'a comedy classic'.*

That did a lot for me, because the fight in script meetings had always been to make it more literal, and while I do believe that there has to be some foundation to make sense of it, the thing that I was most gratified about was that audiences could go along with something that didn't follow what you're constantly getting hammered into your head by the studios, which is: it's got to be literal. *Beetlejuice* proved that it didn't have to be that way. I went through a lot of scary stuff because it didn't test well and they wanted to change the title to make it something more benign, and I fought all that. They wanted to call it *House Ghosts*, and it came very close to being changed. I was at a meeting and they said, '*Beetlejuice* doesn't test, but *House Ghosts* is going through the roof.' As a joke I said, 'Why don't we call it *Scared Sheetless*?' and they actually considered it until I said I'd jump out the window. But to give Warner Bros their due, they left it as it was. They didn't have to, so I was very, very grateful.

If there was one consistent criticism levelled at Beetlejuice *it was that Davis's and Baldwin's characters were boring in comparison with everything else that was going on in the film. It was as if Burton paid more attention to the other characters and the film's design than to them.*

I never saw the Maitlands as one hundred per cent good; they had their problems. The whole gist to me with them was that these are people that like being boring. It's like that thing in old movies where the bland characters need to get goosed a little; they need to get their blood going a little

The Maitlands

bit. Alec kind of bad-mouthed the movie and me and while I think he did a good job, I don't think he saw it for what it was. I don't know what he saw. To me they always were kind of nice, but there was a lot of criticism that they were bland and everything else was great. But if you didn't have those bland characters for Betelgeuse and those afterlife characters to bounce off of, it wouldn't be what it is. That was the point, in a way.

Batman

The movie rights to Bob Kane's comic strip character had been secured from DC Comics in 1979 by producers Benjamin Melniker and Michael Uslan, who had hired Superman screenwriter Tom Mankiewicz to write a script which focused on the Dark Knight's origins. Eventually, Melniker and Uslan relinquished production duties to Peter Guber and Jon Peters, and throughout the early eighties a number of film-makers, including Joe Dante and Ivan Reitman, were linked to the property, though it remained in development until a satisfactory script was found. Following the success of Pee-Wee's Big Adventure, the project, which was in development at Warner Bros, was offered to Burton. His Frankenweenie producer, Julie Hickson, wrote a thirty-page treatment, before Burton brought in Sam Hamm, a comic book fan and screenwriter with only one produced credit, Never Cry Wolf.

They had had the project for ten years and had had several directors attached to it. After Pee-Wee, they asked me if I was interested in directing Batman, and I was. But they didn't give the okay officially until after the first weekend's grosses from Beetlejuice came in. It was kind of charming in a way, because Sam and I would meet on weekends to discuss the early writing stages, and we had a great script, but they kept saying there were other things involved. They were just waiting to see how Beetlejuice did. They didn't want to give me that movie unless Beetlejuice was going to be okay. They wouldn't say that, but that was really the way it was. So, after that first weekend, it got the magical green-light.

Hamm and Burton fashioned a dark, brooding, deeply psychological story for the Caped Crusader which, like Mankiewicz's script, pitted him against The Joker but was set in a dark, hellish vision of Gotham City that eschewed the campness of the Batman TV series of the sixties and instead went back to Kane's original comic strips of the forties. Helping sell Warners on the script's noirish approach was the comic book/graphic

Tim Burton

novel explosion of the mid-eighties, and the resurgence of interest in Batman that had been initiated by comic book artist/writer Frank Miller's The Dark Knight Returns, *a graphic novel which delved into the darker side of Batman's psyche, and Alan Moore's* The Killing Joke, *which featured Batman battling against The Joker.*

I was never a giant comic book fan, but I've always loved the image of Batman and The Joker. The reason I've never been a comic book fan – and I think it started when I was a child – is because I could never tell which box I was supposed to read. That's why I loved *The Killing Joke*, because for the first time I could tell which one to read. It's my favourite. It's the first comic I've ever loved. And the success of those graphic novels made our ideas more acceptable.

So, while I was never a big comic book fan, I loved Batman, the split personality, the hidden person. It's a character I could relate to. Having those two sides, a light side and a dark one, and not being able to resolve them – that's a feeling that's not uncommon. So while I can see it's got a lot of Michael Keaton in it because he's actually doing it, I also see certain aspects of myself in the character. Otherwise, I wouldn't have been able to do it. I mean, this whole split personality thing is so much a part of every person that it's just amazing to me that more people don't consciously understand it. Everybody has several sides to their personality, no one is one thing. Especially in America, people often present themselves as one thing, but are really something else. Which is symbolic of the Batman character.

While the casting of Jack Nicholson as The Joker received almost unanimous acceptance, that of Michael Keaton in the dual role of Bruce Wayne and Batman sparked off an unprecedented amount of controversy. It was producer Jon Peters who first suggested Keaton for the role, and when the news was announced Bat-fans the world over were horrified, with 50,000 letters flooding into Warner Bros' offices to protest at the decision. In fact, the negative reaction reached such proportions that Warners' share price slumped, outraged fans tore up offending publicity material at comic conventions and the Wall Street Journal *covered the crisis on page one. One appalled aficionado wrote in the* Los Angeles Times *that, 'By casting a clown, Warner Bros and Burton have defecated on the history of Batman.' Even Adam West, who had camped up the Caped Crusader in the TV series of the sixties, thought himself a better choice than Keaton.*

In my mind I kept reading reviews that said, 'Jack's terrific, but the unknown as Batman is nothing special.' So I saw a zillion people and the thing that kept going through my mind when I saw these action-adventure hero types come into the office was, 'I just can't see them putting on a bat-suit. I can't see it.' I was seeing these big macho guys, and then thinking of them with pointy eyes, and it was, 'Why would this big, macho, Arnold Schwarzenegger-type person dress up as a bat for God's sake?' A bat is this wild thing. I'd worked with Michael before and so I thought he would be perfect, because he's got that look in his eye. It's there in *Beetlejuice*. It's like *that* guy you could see putting on a bat-suit; he does it because he *needs* to, because he's not this gigantic, strapping macho man. It's all

Adam West: TV's Batman

about transformation. Then it started to make sense to me. All of a sudden the whole thing clicked, I could see the pointy ears; the image and the psychology all made sense. Taking Michael and making him Batman just underscored the whole split personality thing which is really what I think the movie's all about.

With all this controversy, the studio was a little apprehensive. It was like, 'That wasn't what we were thinking.' But they quickly understood.

73

Obviously, there was a lot of negative response from comic book people. I think they thought we were going to make it like the TV series, and make it campy, because they all thought of Michael from *Mr Mom* and *Night Shift* and stuff like that. But that never bothered me because I knew we weren't doing that. Whatever the movie would be, I knew we weren't making a joke of the material.

When I was at school I went to a comic book convention in San Diego a few months before *Superman* was due to be released, and someone from Warner Bros came down and gave a presentation, and the fans tore him to shreds. That was the first time I really saw the intensity and passion that comic book fans have. They didn't like the fact that Superman changed into his costume on the edge of a building. This one guy stood up and said, 'I'm going to boycott this movie and tell everyone you are destroying the legend', and there was this huge round of applause. I never forgot that.

I remember when I first met Bob Kane, he was very pleased with what Sam Hamm and I had done with the script, but he was as freaked out as the rest of them about certain choices in it. Michael Keaton is not the image of Bruce Wayne, but in the comic books the image of The Joker is this really thin so-and-so, so it's a bit elitist to say Jack Nicholson's perfect. Well, he *is* perfect, but he's certainly not the comic book image. So people's bibles seemed to change. If you look at the *Batman* encyclopedia, the fucking thing changes every fucking week. Because, if you think about the reality of it, comic book writers say, 'God, what are we going to do this week? Let's change the history of how Robin was created.' There's no such thing as a bible. I always react against the single-mindedness that you find in Hollywood a lot. You can't think about it. I thought about being true to what I loved about the original idea, and I think in the spirit of it, it's close to Bob Kane. If you look at Michael, he's got all those wheels and that wild energy in his eyes which would compel him to put on a bat-suit. It's like, if he had gotten therapy he wouldn't be putting on a bat-suit. He didn't, so this is his therapy.

But there was no way to satisfy everybody. What you just had to hope for was that you were true to the spirit. And luckily comic books had gone through a phase where they had become much more acceptable. They had made things darker. They had taken Batman into the psychological domain. To me it was very clear: the TV series was campy; the regeneration, the new comics, were totally rebelling against that. I just had to be true to the spirit of it and what I got out of it: the absurdity of it.

Part of what interested me was that it's a human character who dresses up in the most extremely vulgar costumes. The first treatment of *Batman*, the Mankiewicz script, was basically *Superman*, only the names had been changed. It had the same jokey tone, as the story followed Bruce Wayne from childhood through to his beginnings as a crime fighter. They didn't acknowledge any of the freakish nature of it, and I found it the most frightening thing I'd ever read. They didn't acknowledge that he was a man who puts on a costume. They just treated it as if he's doing it for good and that was it. You can't do that. I never felt there had been a totally successful comic book movie ever made. At least not one that I had seen. I thought *Superman* was well done, but in terms of capturing the very specific feel of a comic book, it really didn't do it.

The Mankiewicz script made it more obvious to me that you couldn't treat *Batman* like *Superman*, or treat it like the TV series, because it's a guy dressing up as a bat and no matter what anyone says that's weird. And you've got to go along with that, to some degree. If you want it to be bright and light you either do *Superman* or Cotton Candy Man, you don't do *Batman*.

The TV series was something else, and I grew up on that. I remember running home to be there on opening night on TV. I was prepared. But they'd *done* that, so there was no point in doing that again. And then, as the movie got closer, the comic book explosion clicked in, which I thought was very healthy for everybody because comics, even though I still didn't really read them, are part of American mythology.

Batman *was filmed at Pinewood Studios in England during the winter of 1988/9 where the entire backlot was turned, at a cost of $5.5 million, into a vision of Gotham City that was described in Sam Hamm's script as 'if Hell had sprung up through the pavements and kept on going'. The man responsible was British production designer Anton Furst, who had previously worked on* The Company of Wolves *and* Full Metal Jacket, *and who Burton had tried to employ for* Beetlejuice.

To do a big movie you either do it in LA or you do it in London, due basically to the facilities. I mean, the dollar wasn't even great at the time, but at Pinewood there was nothing going on and it had a big outdoor area which we could build on. So it made sense. The characters were so extreme that I felt we had to set them somewhere that was designed for them. Because *Superman* had been filmed on New York locations, I don't think it captured the right comic book feel. I was very happy we did it at

Pinewood, just to get away from all that stuff with the casting and the hype and the pressure. The British press were intense too, but that didn't bother me as much. I liked being there, I liked working there, I liked a lot of the people, a lot of great artists; I made some friends and it was nice.

Design is very important to me and there are very few designers that I get excited about. Anton was a great designer. I had liked *The Company of Wolves*, and I thought he was one of the most individual ones around. I had met him before *Beetlejuice* and tried to get him to work on that, but he was working on something else. Because of my background, design is the one area I'm very critical about. Working with someone like Anton, who had a real talent, is a luxury. It excites me and it has always been important for me to like designers as friends.

For Gotham City we looked at pictures of New York. *Blade Runner* had come out, and any time there's a movie like that, that's such a trend setter, you're in danger. We had said early on that any city we were going to do was going to get the inevitable *Blade Runner* comparison. So we decided there was nothing we could do about it. We just said, 'This is what's happening to New York at the moment. Things are being added and built on and design is getting all over the place.' We decided to darken everything and build vertically and cram things together and then just go further with it in a more cartoon way. It has an operatic feel, and an almost timeless quality, which I think is similar to *Beetlejuice*.

Every time I do anything I start with the character. Batman's character likes the dark and wants to remain in the shadows, so it's a city at night without many day scenes. Everything is meant to support these characters, so every decision we make is based on that, running it by the character almost, and making sure it's okay with what that character's about.

In addition to the casting of Keaton, comic book fans were also outraged by the redesign of the bat-suit by costume designer Bob Ringwood, who changed its colour from blue to black and incorporated fake musculature into the design.

We just took off from the psychology of saying 'Here's a guy who doesn't look like Arnold Schwarzenegger, so why is he doing this?' He's trying to create an image for himself, he's trying to become something that he's not. Therefore, every decision that we made was based upon that. What's he trying to achieve? Why do you dress up as a bat? You're trying to scare criminals, you're putting on a show, you are trying to

Batman: the image

scare and intimidate people. The idea was to humanize the character.

Despite Warners' initial faith in Hamm's screenplay, the script went through another two writers – Beetlejuice's Warren Skaaren and Charles McKeown, co-writer of Terry Gilliam's The Adventures of Baron Münchausen *– and also required rewrites on set.*

I don't understand why that became such a problem. We started out with a script that everyone liked, although we recognized it needed a little work. Everyone thought the script was great, but they *still* thought it needed a total rewrite. Obviously it was a big movie, and it represented an enormous investment by Warners, so I understood why we had to make it right. But what made the situation worse was that there was all this fuss about making the script better and suddenly we were shooting.

There were so many changes and fixes that it was like unravelling a ball of yarn. It gets to a point where you're *not* helping it any more. We were shooting a scene leading up to the bell-tower and Jack's walking up the steps, but we didn't know why. He said to me that day, 'Why am I going up the steps?' And I said, 'I don't know, we'll talk about it when you get up the top.' You're always working on something, you're always trying to make it better, that happens all the way through, but in this case I felt I wasn't making it better. That pressure is really lousy because you don't have your own strong foundation to stand on like you usually do. I like improvising, but not that way. *Beetlejuice* was amorphous, but it didn't matter because it wasn't as expensive, and it wasn't as big a dinosaur.

The first time you direct a movie on that scale it's kind of surreal. You're not fearful because you don't know. You only have to fight things off after you've been through it once or twice. It's a weird kind of conditioning. If you give somebody a little electrical jolt, the first time they won't know what's coming. After that, they'll be thinking about that little jolt. It's a similar kind of thing.

I was very lucky because I didn't go into it with a fear of 'Oh my God, Jack Nicholson!' And he was great to me. He was very supportive. With Jack a lot of the work was done early on in terms of how he felt about me. He was very cool. He helped me a lot when there was trouble on the movie and the studio freaked out. He was very calming and helpful and would just say, 'Get what you need, get what you want, and just keep going.' He's so great. He'll do like six takes and each take he'll give it

The Joker

Batman: 'The duel of the freaks'

something else. He was fascinating that way, and you'd almost wish you could play all six takes in the movie. He was very exciting to watch.

Charles McKeown came in and we did some work on The Joker character. He was The Joker and he needed more jokes, not for the sake of more jokes, but because that was his character. He needed more of that identification. He's the best character and besides Catwoman he's the clearest villain. I just love the idea of a person who's turned into a clown and is insane. The film is like the duel of the freaks. It's a fight between two disfigured people. That's what I love about it. I was always aware of how weird it was, but I was never worried about it in any way. The Joker is such a great character because there's a complete freedom to him. Any character who operates on the outside of society and is deemed a freak and an outcast then has the freedom to do what they want. The Joker and Beetlejuice can do that in a much more liberating way than, say, Edward Scissorhands, or even Pee-Wee, because they're deemed disgusting. They are the darker sides of freedom. Insanity is in some scary way the most freedom you can have, because you're not bound by the laws of society.

We tried to put Robin in, to make that relationship work in a real way. In the TV series he's just *there*. We tried a slightly more psychological approach, but I felt unless you're going to focus on that and give it its due, it's like 'Who is this guy?' Sam and I spent a lot of time going over that, anguishing over it. It's a good thing we didn't do it, because it would have cost a lot, and when we were getting ready to shoot the movie it was the easiest lift. Again, I just went back to the psychology of a man who dresses up as a bat; he's a very singular, lonely character, and putting him with somebody just didn't make sense. It didn't make sense in the next one either; we tried it there too. But it's just too much. There's too much material with these characters.

As with Pee-Wee's Big Adventure *and* Beetlejuice, *Burton called upon Danny Elfman to provide* Batman's *dark, orchestral score. This time, however, Elfman's soundtrack album was complemented by one from Prince, who had initially been commissioned to provide two songs for the movie.*

We needed two numbers – one for when The Joker goes into the museum, and the other for the parade sequence, and I actually used music by Prince for those scenes when we shot them. But what happened was it snowballed. It got bigger. He really got into the movie and wrote a bunch of songs. Guber and Peters had this idea of getting Michael Jackson to do the love theme, Prince to do The Joker theme, and Danny would just tie it all together. They can make that work for *Top Gun*, but my stuff isn't like that. It needs to be finessed a bit more. And I don't think those songs work. It doesn't have anything to do with Prince's music, it has more to do with their integration into the film. I liked them on their own, but I'm not proficient enough to make something like that work if it's not right.

I love Prince. I saw him twice at Wembley when I was shooting the movie. I think he's incredible. Here was a guy who was looking at a movie and doing his thing to it. It's like what comic book people do, it's their impression. I love that. I wish there was more of that kind of thing. It's cool to have crossover things like that. But I couldn't make the songs work, and I think I did a disservice to the movie and to him. But the record company wanted those things to be in there. Obviously, they made a lot of money from it, so I guess in that respect they achieved something. But I don't feel I made it work very well. The songs bring it too much into a specific time frame.

Batman *opened in the USA on 21 June 1989 and became the first film to* *break $100 million in its first ten days of release. It eventually became not only the top money-maker of 1989, with a worldwide gross in excess of $500 million, and the biggest film in Warner Bros's history, but also a multi-media merchandising and cultural phenomenon, the hype of which had never been seen before; until the release of* Jurassic Park *in 1993, it was the blockbuster against which all subsequent blockbusters had to be measured.*

The interesting thing about hype is that everyone thought the studio was creating it, when in fact you can't create hype; it's a phenomenon that's beyond a studio, it has a life of its own. The most negative thing to me was working on something that gained so much hype, because I'm the type of person – and there is a percentage of the population out there like myself – who if I hear too much about something gets turned off by it. And it was odd to be working on something that, if I was a normal person, I'd have gone, 'Shut the fuck up. I'm sick of hearing about this thing. I won't go see it, 'cos I've heard too much about it.' That was the most disturbing thing. But there was no way to control it. And then you get the inevitable backlash to that. My main concern was that the movie be judged on its own merits and not become this *thing*. But there's nothing you can do about it. It helped being in England, even with the press attention there, because it wasn't my country, and so I just focused on making the movie and didn't think too much about anything else.

Batman *won Anton Furst an Oscar for his design work, but was criticized in some quarters for being 'too dark'. Many critics also felt that Burton was more interested in The Joker than in the title character.*

That's not true, but there is an inherent problem with these characters. It was similar to the criticism that Adam and Barbara Maitland were boring. That's not true either. But there is an inherent difference in the characters of Batman and The Joker: The Joker is an extrovert and Batman an introvert. So no matter what you do, you can't match the energy, the balance. You have this character who always wants to remain in the shadows, to remain hidden. If these two were standing on the street, Batman would always be wanting to hide, whereas The Joker would be, 'Look at me. Look at me.' So that's part of what the energy of it was. I certainly wasn't less interested in Batman, it's just that he is who he is, and The Joker is who he is. Right or wrong, I sort of let these things play themselves out.

Some people got it, some people understood that. Obviously, a lot of people thought The Joker was the thing, but a lot of people found Michael to be more compelling because of that. He captured a certain subtle sadness in his character. It was as if he was thinking, 'Look at this guy. He gets to go out there and jump around and be a clown, and I have to remain in the shadows.' And there was a pent-up, bottled-up feeling to him which I think works with the Batman character.

It's funny, that whole dark and light thing. In fact, I've gotten more confused by it in a way. It was so weird on the second *Batman* because I would do those big press junkets where you're seeing a zillion people – every six minutes somebody new – and it became like a joke. I felt I was on *Candid Camera*, because one person would come in and go, 'The film is much lighter than the last one', and then the next person would come up and say, 'It's much darker than the first movie.' I felt like a psycho because I never think of things as dark or light. I've always felt that you couldn't even pull apart light and dark, they're so intertwined. I felt that way growing up, and I feel that way now. Sometimes I'll watch something that people don't see anything weird about and I'll find it deeply subversive and scary and dark. And then people will look at something that I've done and go, 'That's really dark', and I don't see it. It's like the end of *Vincent* when they said they wanted him to live and walk off with his dad. That felt darker to me, because the other ending felt more beautiful and more like what was in his mind, which is what the thing was about. It was about somebody's spirit, and to make it literal was, I felt, making it darker, ultimately. So what is perceived as light and dark is completely open to interpretation.

During the shooting of Batman, *Burton met Lena Gieseke, a German painter, and they were married in February 1989 while he was completing post-production in England.*

Edward Scissorhands

Following the enormous success of Batman, *Burton was considered
Hollywood's hottest young director. But rather than direct the* Batman
sequel that Warner Bros wanted, he opted to make Edward Scissorhands,
*a film he had long cherished, and one based on an image – a man with
scissors in place of hands – that he had been toying with since childhood.
Though Burton had been linked with Warners for his previous three films,
he found the studio unreceptive to the idea, and sought out another studio
which would allow him the freedom to make the film his way. He found it
in Twentieth Century-Fox, which was then being run by former director
Joe Roth.*

Warners just didn't get it, which was good because I knew they didn't
want to do it. I try to work with people who want to do what I want to
do. Even now I try to gauge if people just want to do it because of me, or
if they actually like it. It's helpful if they respond to the material because
it's such a difficult process. So it was for the best, I think, because
Warners weren't into it. Hollywood is so strange, though; for a community made up of so many freakish outsiders, it's oddly conservative.

Even though I have come up through the studio system, I haven't really felt like I have, and I don't think the studio people feel like I have
either; they sometimes look at me with a sort of worried expression,
often about what it is I want to do. But there's a great energy about that
too, there's something that's great about operating within that system
and then approaching things the way you want to. There's kind of a perverse charm to it.

Back when Burton had been in pre-production on Beetlejuice, *he had commissioned Caroline Thompson, a young novelist, to write the screenplay
for* Edward Scissorhands. *The pair had been introduced through their
agent who thought they might get on. He was right. In Thompson, Burton
found a kindred spirit who would later write the screenplay for another of*

Johnny Depp as Edward Scissorhands

Burton's long-cherished projects, The Nightmare Before Christmas.

I had read her book, *First Born*, which was about an abortion that came
back to life. It was good. It had sociological things that were thematic, but
also had fantastical elements to it, which was nice, and the combination of

85

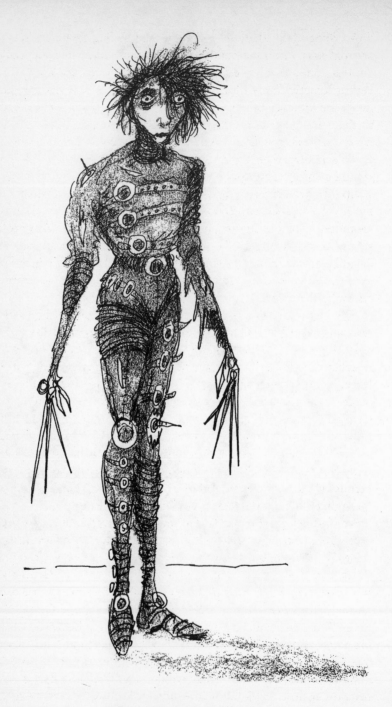

Edward Scissorhands

those things I liked. It was close to the feeling I wanted for *Edward Scissorhands*. I'm not the most communicative of people, especially when an idea comes from a feeling, so I was lucky to meet Caroline. She was very in tune with my ideas, which was good because the idea had been inside me for a long time, it was symbolic and not something I wanted to sit there and pick apart and analyse. I needed somebody who understood what the basic thing was about, so there wouldn't have to be a lot of grade school psychology going on in terms of discussing the project. I could be fairly cryptic and it still came across to her.

I paid Caroline a few thousand dollars to write it so there was no studio involved. That was good. Sometimes you just like to get it out. We submitted it to the studios as a package. It was like, 'Okay, this is the script. This is the movie. Do you guys wanna do it?' There wasn't a lot of haggling around about it, which is the best way to get anything done. We gave them two weeks to say yes or no. It was a route I was determined to follow so that no one could force changes on me.

The idea actually came from a drawing I did a long time ago. It was just an image that I liked. It came subconsciously and was linked to a character who wants to touch but can't, who was both creative and destructive – those sort of contradictions can create a kind of ambivalence. It was very much linked to a feeling. The manifestation of the image made itself apparent and probably came to the surface when I was a teenager, because it is a very teenage thing. It had to do with relationships. I just felt I couldn't communicate. It was the feeling that your image and how people perceive you are at odds with what is inside you, which is a fairly common feeling. I think a lot of people feel that way to some degree, because it's frustrating and sad to feel a certain way but for it not to come through. So the idea had to do with image and perception.

I remember growing up and feeling that there is not a lot of room for acceptance. You are taught at a very early age to conform to certain things. It's a situation, at least in America, that's very prevalent and which starts from day one at school: this person's smart, this person's not smart, this person's good at sports, this one's not, this person's weird, this one's normal. From day one you're categorized. That was the strongest impulse in the film. I remember sitting there as a child, looking at the teacher saying some other kid is stupid, and really he's not stupid, he's much more intelligent than a lot of others and has a lot more spirit, it's just that he's not conforming to the teacher's image. So I think the film is more of a reaction against that kind of categorization. I fell into the weird category because I was quiet, I was interiorized. People are categorized very easily,

Edward suburbanized

even in Hollywood. I talk to actors all the time who are categorized as dramatic and so can't do this or that. I don't know why people do it because it seems to me that nobody would like it done to them. It's kind of sad and frustrating at the same time, because somebody's saying you're this and somehow it's removed from you. And the more quiet somebody is, or the more different people feel you are, the more they like to do it.

On the surface Edward Scissorhands *appeared to be yet another of Burton's reworkings of* Frankenstein. *Edward, the unfinished creation of his inventor/father who dies before he can complete the job, is removed from his lonely existence in a hilltop castle by Avon lady Peg Boggs (Dianne Wiest) and finds himself living with her family in a pastel-coloured version of suburbia. There he becomes the source of fantasy, gossip, resentment, adoration and lust for the neighbours, who he wins over with his wildly kitsch topiaries, outlandish hairstyles and elaborate ice sculptures.*

First came the image, linked to those feelings of not being accepted. Then from that came the images of the ice and the hedges, just as a natural out-

Edward meets the Avon Lady (Johnny Depp and Dianne Wiest)

Edward and the hedges

growth of him being a helpful, handy household item. And then there was the world that he comes into; that came more from my memory of growing up in that world, in suburbia, and the feelings that were linked to it. Memory has a way of heightening itself. Any time you think back to something, the further away it is, the more extreme, the more heightened it becomes. The interesting thing about these neighbourhoods is that they're so close together you know everybody, but there's stuff underneath that you just don't know. Sexual stuff. There's a certain kind of kinkiness to suburbia. There was an undercurrent of it when I was growing up. I never saw it specifically, but you certainly got a feeling of it.

I grew up in suburbia and I still don't understand certain aspects of it. There's a certain kind of vagueness, a blankness, and I got this very strongly from my family. The pictures my family had on the walls, I never got the sense that they liked them, that they bought them, that somebody had given them to them. It was almost as if they had always been there, and yet no one had ever looked at them. I remember sitting there looking at some of these things going, 'What the hell is that? What are those resin grapes? Where did they get them? What does it mean?'

Growing up in suburbia was like growing up in a place where there's no sense of history, no sense of culture, no sense of passion for anything.

You never felt people liked music. There was no showing of emotion. It was very strange. 'Why is that there? What am I sitting on?' You never felt that there was any attachment to things. So you were either forced to conform and cut out a large portion of your personality, or to develop a very strong interior life which made you feel separate.

But the film is not autobiographical, because it was important for me to be as objective as possible. That's why I felt very lucky to have Johnny because he brought to it a lot of themes that are nearer his life which, when I started to talk to him, I liked very much. I could look at him and draw upon his world, in a way.

Johnny Depp, star of TV's teen detective show 21 Jump Street *and John Waters's* Cry-Baby, *had always been Burton's number one choice for the role of Edward Scissorhands, although he had initially met Tom Cruise in connection with the part.*

They are always saying, here is a list of five people who are box-office, and three of them are Tom Cruise. I've learned to be open at the initial stage and talk to people. He certainly wasn't my ideal, but I talked to him. He was interesting, but I think it worked out for the best. A lot of questions came up – I don't really recall the specifics – but at the end of the meeting I did feel like, and I probably even said this to him, 'It's nice to have a lot of questions about the character, but you either do it or you don't do it.'

I was glad Johnny did it. I can't think of anybody else who would have done it for me that way. I didn't really know him. I hadn't seen that TV show he'd been in, but I must have seen a picture of him somewhere. I like people's eyes a lot and, especially with a character like this who doesn't really speak, eyes are very important. We wanted him right from the beginning, but I was open about meeting other people because I think when I first started out I was a little snobby about the whole thing. I was, 'I don't like that person, I don't like this person', and sometimes I'd meet people and they were different from what I'd expected. So I've tried to become more open, because you can be surprised that way.

In America, Johnny is very much known as a teen idol and he's perceived as difficult and aloof; there are all sorts of things written about him in the press which are completely untrue. I mean, as a person he's a very funny, warm, great guy. He's a normal guy – at least my interpretation of normal – but he's perceived as dark and difficult and weird, and is judged by his looks. But he's almost completely the opposite of this perception. So the themes of *Edward*, of image and perception, of somebody being perceived to be the opposite of what he is, was a theme he could relate to. The words 'freakish' and 'freak' have so many interpretations, and in a weird way he sort of relates to freaks because he's treated as one. That flip-flopping and inverting of themes and perceptions was something he really responded to because he goes through that all the time. You pick up a tabloid and he's portrayed as the brooding James Dean type or whatever way people want to label him as, but he's not. People get judged by their looks a lot. It's fascinating; it's always been that way and it probably always will be. It's sad when you're judged by the way you look, and that sadness builds up in you because, at least for me, there was always a desire to connect with people – not everybody, but some people, one or two – and he's probably been through a lot of that kind of stuff, so he understood that side of it.

I think that a lot of the character is him. He has this kind of naïve quality which as you get older gets tested and has holes poked into it. It's hard to maintain that, because you don't want to shield yourself from society and the rest of the world completely, but at the same time you'd like to maintain a certain kind of openness and feeling that you had earlier on in your life. And I would imagine Johnny is somebody who would want to protect that to some degree.

Playing opposite Depp as Wiest's cheerleader daughter, Kim, was Winona Ryder, who had made such an impact in Beetlejuice, *and who, at the time, was romantically involved with her co-star.*

I like her very much. She's one of my favourites. Also she responds to this kind of dark material and I thought the idea of her as a cheerleader, wearing a blonde wig, was very funny. I think she might even say it's probably the most difficult thing she's ever done because she did not relate to her character. She was tortured by these people at school herself. It was so funny. I used to laugh every day when I saw her walk on the set wearing this little cheerleader outfit and a Hayley Mills-type blonde wig. She looked liked Bambi.

I don't think their relationship affected the movie in a negative way. Perhaps it might have if it had been a different kind of movie, something that was tapping more into some positive or negative side of their relationship. But this was such a fantasy. The fact that we were in Florida

Kim (Winona Ryder) and the ice

probably was helpful for the two of them to be together, because it was a pretty bizarre environment. But they were very professional and didn't bring any weird stuff to the set.

Everybody goes down to Florida for the weather. It's like a joke. I went there partially as a desire to get away from Hollywood and partially because the type of suburban neighbourhoods in California in which the film takes place were built in the fifties and they've all got very overgrown now. And Florida just happened to be a place where the neighbourhoods were new and had that flavour to them.

In typically Burtonesque fashion, the houses in this particular suburbia were slightly removed from reality by being painted various pastel shades.

It was seen from Edward's point of view, a slightly more romanticized view of the world. I like dark colours better, but they weren't too dissimilar from what was already there. And although the production designer Bo Welch painted all the houses different colours, it was important to me that the area still remain a community. We hardly touched the insides of the houses. What you see is pretty much what was there.

Sometimes people say, 'Are you going to do a real film with real people?' But to me the words 'normal' and 'real' have a thousand different interpretations. What's real? What's normal? And I think the reason I like fairy tales so much as a form – at least my interpretation of the form – what I get out of fairy tales, folk tales, myths, are these very extreme images, very heightened, but with some foundation to them. It means something, but is fairly abstract and if it's going to connect with you it will connect with you, and if it's not then it won't. I think that's the danger, especially in commercial film-making, because sometimes things will just leave people cold, it's not literal enough. A question they ask is 'Where did Edward get the ice?' Go see *Three Men and a Little Lady* if that's your thing. There's a certain amount of symbolism, a certain amount of interpretation and abstraction which I appreciate. I much prefer to connect with something on a subconscious level than to intellectualize about it. I prefer to intellectualize about it slightly after the fact.

I don't follow any script like the Bible because it changes in the process of the visualization of it. It is a different thing. I get out of a script the things I need. It's constantly changing, it's organic. So I just try to take the root and spirit of it. Sometimes I'll think there's a great line in a script, and then when a certain actor says it, it just doesn't come across. Whereas another actor could maybe say the line a better way. It's very much down to the elements involved at the moment you're doing it. Sometimes things just mutate. There's an excitement about that that I like. I don't mind if things change a little, I don't mind seeing how things work out, even from when you're shooting it, to when you see it on film. I remember Johnny was able to do something that amazed me. I was very close to him one day, watching him doing a scene, and the next day we saw it on film, and almost without doing anything he was able to do something with his eyes that made them glassy. It was as if he was about to cry, like one of those Walter Keane paintings with the big eyes. I don't know how he did it. It wasn't something we did with the camera or the lighting, it was incredible and that kind of excitement – weird little things, weird new images that surprise you – is very specific to film.

I love actors like Johnny and Dianne Wiest and Alan Arkin who are really doing a lot under the surface and doing a lot for the other characters; they're very unselfish. Those are the things that I enjoy the most when I see the movies years later. Dianne, in particular, was wonderful. She was the first actress to read the script, supported it completely and, because she is so respected, once she had given it her stamp of approval, others soon got interested. In many ways, she was my guardian angel.

Edward's isolation

In the film, Ryder's cheerleader, Kim, leaves her jock boyfriend, played by Anthony Michael Hall, to be with Edward, an event that many have postulated as Burton's revenge against those jocks he encountered at school.

I was always amazed by those guys in school. I would sit there thinking to myself: they've always got the girlfriends, they're always the image of things, and yet these guys are psychotic. If she stays with him, they'll get married straight out of high school, and he'll end up beating her up. It'll be that kind of situation. I resisted those kinds of labels because what others perceived to be the norm, often turned out to be the opposite. It's funny, I went back to a high school reunion and it was true – and this is pretty much across the board – that the people who were considered outcasts and freaks at high school – much more than me; I was considered quiet, so I sort of remained out of everything, but some people were really tortured – these people ended up being the most well-adjusted, really attractive (not just physically but attractive as people) and were doing really well. And the other people had faded. The presidents, the jocks, they had truly peaked in high school, and it was so shocking to

The Avon lady enters Edward's domain

see that. It confirmed your suspicions about things, because those who were tortured were forced to be their own people; they couldn't rely on society, they couldn't rely on the culture or the hierarchy to take care of them, so to speak, so they had to make themselves acceptable.

Hall's jock is subsequently killed, a scene that shocked a number of people who felt the whole tone of the movie had been radically altered.

That was perhaps some sort of junior high or high school revenge fantasy, I guess, somewhere deep inside. I don't know, perhaps I was just letting off steam.

In the small but pivotal role of Edward's inventor/father, Burton cast Vincent Price, with whom he had maintained a friendship since they worked together on Vincent.

When he did this, even though it was a small role, it had a lot of emotional impact for me, because he looks so amazing. When I see it and see him, it gives me a strong feeling. There are lots of layers of symbols and

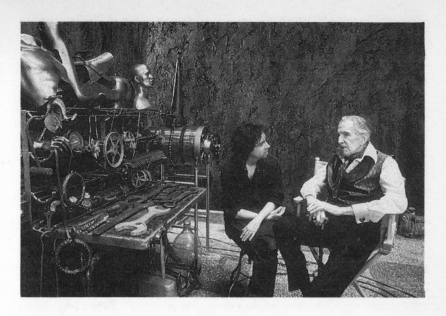

Tim Burton and Vincent Price

Edward Scissorhands and his inventor/father

themes; his role probably had a lot to do with how I felt about him in terms of watching his movies and how he was my mentor, so to speak, through the movies. I was very happy that he did it and I got to know him a little better. After *Vincent* we had struck up a friendship, and I had always kept in touch with him, even loosely, when I was away in England making *Batman*. It was nice for me, because he was of the generation that, even if you didn't keep in touch regularly, you kept connected to in some way. He was really great that way.

After completing Edward Scissorhands *Burton began directing a documentary on his idol, who died in 1993, entitled* Conversations with Vincent *(working title).*

I knew he wasn't well. He hadn't been well ever since his wife died right after we were shooting the documentary. He was really into her and maybe the impulse to join her was there. I was sad. It's a loss, but he was an incredible person who had given a lot.

Depp's Edward is found living alone in the attic of a gothic castle, two settings that have regularly been the dwelling place of numerous Burton characters.

There's a sense of isolation in that. Symbolically I associate it with isolation. But it's also a reaction against the suburban home in some ways. It's like, if you've grown up and lived your whole life in one of those, you start imagining all sorts of things as a reaction against that. It was always a desire to be up, or out, or away, and in an environment that was not white like being inside a shoe box.

Edward Scissorhands *climaxes, much like James Whale's* Frankenstein, *and indeed much like Burton's own* Frankenweenie, *with a mob confronting the 'evil creature' – in this case, Edward – at his castle.*

Again, when you grow up watching these things you make analogies to your own life. I had always felt that growing up in those kinds of neighbourhoods the only time you'd ever see the neighbours all together was if there was an accident or something out front. Then the pull-out-the-lawnchairs kind of mob mentality would kick in. I was always fascinated by that, and how the parallel between suburban life and a horror movie was really closer than you might think. The mob mentality is in a lot of those horror movies.

With Edward Scissorhands finally unable to consummate his love for Kim because of his appearance, the film can also be seen as Burton's version of Beauty and the Beast, *a fairy-tale bookended by a prologue and an epilogue featuring Winona Ryder as an old woman telling her granddaughter the story of Edward.*

That's such a classic theme. Someone said there were only five stories, well, that's one of them. It's a theme that's in thousands of stories and any number of horror pictures. Obviously, I was conscious of it in a thematic way, but it's simply *there*, it's not something I dwelled on very much. It wasn't the overriding impulse to do the film, but it certainly was a part of it.

To create Edward's scissor hands, Burton employed Oscar-winning special effects artist Stan Winston, who would later go on to design The Penguin's make-up for Batman Returns.

Stan's the greatest. I love Stan. And part of his success is that he knows how to deal with people. A lot of people who do effects are very hard to communicate with. Stan's got such a big operation, and he's got a lot of great people working with him. He knows how to deal with me. He tries to get into the spirit of it, which is great. I give him my cheesy little sketches and he goes from there. I'm always appreciative of people who like to look at them, because obviously you can't just take my sketches and make them, there's another very crucial step where they're transformed into reality with an actor. But Stan would look at them and take them and do some illustrations and stuff. It was just a real pleasure. And he's got the cleanest studio I've ever seen in my life. I've never seen a cleaner special effects place. I used to joke with him about it because there's something wrong with that. It's like a museum. Everybody else's place, except for Rick Baker's, looks like my place, like a dump.

   The scissor hands had to be large since I wanted Johnny to be beautiful and dangerous. We made him a pair and let him put them on and try to do something, and he learned better than just rehearsing what the feeling is like. Again, it was a case of becoming the character.

In 1989 Burton formed Tim Burton Productions with Denise Di Novi, a former journalist and the producer of Heathers, *as president of the company. Together they produced* Edward Scissorhands, Batman Returns *and* The Nightmare Before Christmas *before Di Novi left the company in 1992, though she has continued to work with Burton, co-producing* Ed Wood *and* Cabin Boy. Edward Scissorhands *marked Burton's first film as producer.*

Even when I wasn't really a producer, when you're doing something that you care about, those lines get very blurred. There's a little bit more responsibility to it, but it's not something that feels that different. A lot of it has to do with your attitude and how you go into something. If you go into something one hundred per cent, it doesn't matter if you're the director/producer. It doesn't feel that different from when you're directing it, anyway.

Denise produced *Ed Wood*, but we've kind of split off a little bit. She's doing more things because I just want to focus on the things that I want to do and not do a whole bunch of other stuff necessarily. I needed somebody to help out and run things. Whereas at the beginning nobody pays any attention to you, once you get a little bit into it you find you're managing an office, because you get submissions, people calling, all that kind of stuff. I was looking to create some sort of semi-solid kind of thing. It's nice to have somebody who's with you, and who's just thinking about you.

Burton oversaw the transfer of Beetlejuice *into a children's cartoon TV series and made his first on screen appearance in Cameron Crowe's twenty-something movie,* Singles, *in which he played a director of dating agency videos referred to as 'the next Martin Scorsese'.*

That guy Cameron asked me to do it. He's a nice guy, and I just did it. I'd never done something like that before and I got to go to Seattle and that was fun. I was curious to see what it would be like to be a cheesy actor, and I certainly was.

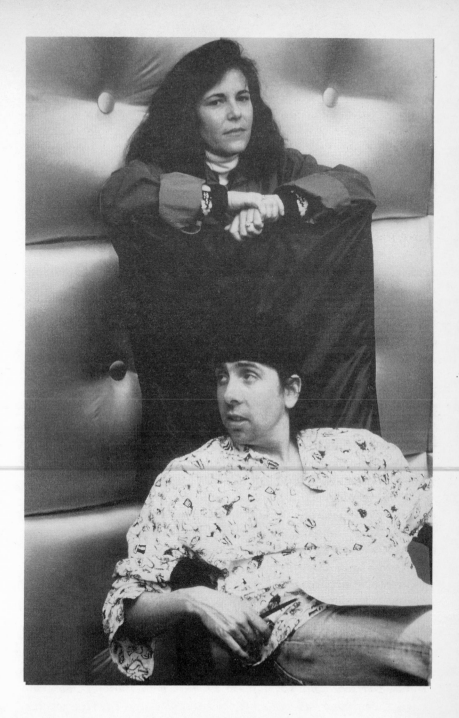

Tim Burton with Denise Di Novi

Batman Returns

While Burton was in Europe promoting the release of Edward Scissorhands, *he admitted that* Batman *was the one movie of his that he didn't feel close to and when, in 1991, he finally decided to direct the sequel, it was to enable him to connect with the material again.*

I didn't want to do the *Batman* sequel initially because I was kind of burnt out, and I didn't know what I could bring to it. It took me a long time to get interested in it again. Part of it was all those big weird circumstances: like not having a minute, working seven days a week under really harsh conditions, not having a chance to think, not having the script sorted out. It's the one movie that I feel more detached from than the others. I think any director will say that the first big movie you do is a little bit of a shock. But again, some of it has to do with how you feel at the time. I never walk into anything without feeling close to it; I *did* originally feel close to it, but it got away from me a little bit. That's how I felt at the time, but now, as everything gets further away, I get a slightly more romanticized vision of it: 'Oh those were the good old days, the first *Batman*.' So when I talked to you I was still suffering from that post-movie depression.

I think every movie that I've done has lots of flaws, it's just that I don't mind the flaws in the others as much as I mind the ones in *Batman*. I treat my films like my mutated children, in a way. They may have flaws, they may have weird problems, but I still love them. It takes me a good three years before I can distance myself from a film and then judge it. It wasn't until a couple of years ago that I could start to enjoy *Pee-Wee's Big Adventure*. The further away a movie is, the clearer it gets, and the more I enjoy it.

Initially Sam Hamm, screenwriter of Batman, *was hired to write* Batman Returns, *but when his script failed to meet with Burton's approval, Daniel Waters, who had written the mordant black comedy* Heathers *for Di Novi, was brought on board.*

Sam wrote one script, but the thing that started to get my interest going was the idea of Catwoman. I talked to Dan Waters loosely about it and he nailed Catwoman very quickly. And I realized I really like this material: I like Batman, I like Catwoman, I like The Penguin, I like their world. It's a good canvas of characters. I like their duality. And the thing that I really liked about *Batman* as a comic book property was that they're all fucked-up characters – that's what's so beautiful about them. Unlike other comics, they're just all fucked, the villains and Batman. But that's also part of the problem – I never see these people as villains.

Waters's script took off from Hamm's original and exploited Batman's vulnerabilities in a devilishly demented plot that pitted him against Catwoman, a PVC-clad anti-heroine engaged in a lust-hate relationship with the Dark Knight; The Penguin, a dark, mutated, nasty half-animal who was disposed of into the sewers as a baby by parents horrified at his flippers; and Max Shreck, the white-haired power-crazed industrialist who essentially acts as the catalyst for all the others. For many, however, it was a case of too many villains spoiling the Batman, with Keaton again forced to take a back seat.

I know. I think I probably got a little carried away. I just found interest in all of them, and I think I kind of evened them all out. I also wanted to have fun on the movie. I didn't have fun on the first one, and I wanted to get back to the feeling I had when I worked on *Beetlejuice*. But it certainly didn't turn out that way; it was the hardest one.

A lot of those characters from the comic strip – The Joker, Catwoman, Harvey Dent – are all very easy to identify in psychological profile. But characters like The Penguin and The Riddler are not so easy. It's like 'Who are these people?' Again, the idea of not knowing who you are, is, I think, why I like the Batman material. It's a very questioning kind of thing: who are we? Is what we perceive reality? But that's a dangerous kind of subject matter because it's very ethereal in some ways. So, we tried to give The Penguin a foundation and a psychological profile. I probably gave it too much, spent too much time on it. But I don't think there's anybody better than Danny at making the horrible acceptable.

I liked the fact that some people couldn't decide whether or not Catwoman was bad. She never was bad. When they were bad on the TV series they were never really bad. That's the thing, I never saw any of them as bad, and I never believe it when they say people are bad. I don't have that compass.

In the dual role of Selina Kyle, Max Shreck's mousy secretary who is transformed into Catwoman in a quite wondrously Burtonesque moment where she receives the life-force out of a number of alleycats, Burton initially cast Annette Benning, who had to bow out after falling pregnant. For Burton there was only one other choice for the role: Michelle Pfeiffer. But Sean Young, who had been cast in the part eventually played by Kim Basinger in the original Batman *until she broke her arm in a riding accident, believed the role should have gone to her and turned up on the Warner Bros lot dressed as Catwoman.*

She came to the studio and into my office. I wasn't there, but she had somebody out in the parking lot, a bodyguard or assistant, and when she saw somebody who looked like me she said, 'There he is, grab him.' I guess it was the publicist of the movie and it freaked him out. Then the people in my office told her it wasn't me, and she stormed over to Mark Canton's office where Michael Keaton was, and demanded to be in the film. After that she went on all these talk shows citing 'unfair Hollywood', which was so absurd, because the simple fact is that casting is just a choice. I'm not 'horrible Hollywood'. I'm not shunning her. But she made it into this big deal, which was absurd. She went on *The Joan Rivers Show* dressed as Catwoman, though her outfit seemed more appropriate for a female wrestling movie from what I saw, and said, 'Horrible Hollywood bigwigs wouldn't see me.' I hated being perceived in that way. I'm very sensitive when it comes to casting. I'm not the type of director who has mindless meetings with people. I don't like putting people through things; I don't want to waste their time. She made it into a big, stupid issue. I think she always wanted to play Catwoman, which is fine, it's a great role. I'd like to play Catwoman, but unfortunately it's just a simple choice and it's my choice, and it doesn't have anything to do with right or wrong. She's screaming 'Hollywood system' and I'm saying 'No, artistic choice'.

I met with Michelle. I hadn't really seen her in very much, but we had a nice meeting and I liked her. Certainly, you can look at Michelle and see she has a feline quality that you would expect in Catwoman, but I just met her and liked her. Again, that's all it is. It's a simple choice, a connection. She was into it. She's from Orange County, a kind of similar era and similar environment to mine and maybe I connected with her on that level. She's a talented actress and did great. I was impressed with her physical talents, the things that she could do. She was game for weird things; she put birds in her mouth, she endured a lot. She also did that weird thing with her eyes. It's not that shocking – given that these people

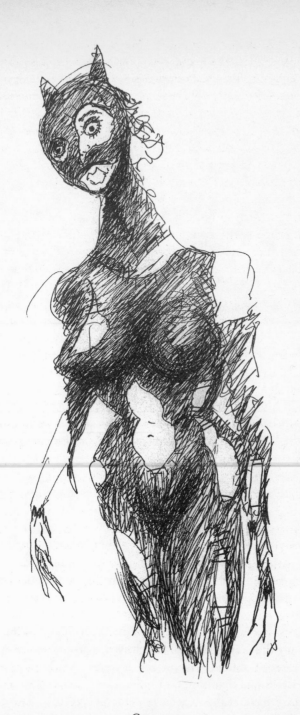

Catwoman

105

Michelle Pfeiffer: 'She has a feline quality'

are covered up with masks – that eyes play such an important part.

In tune with Burton's fascination with duality, the film is full of warped tensions, deep, dark dialogue and remarkably complex characters whose other sides Burton twists into a bitter confection, with Batman and Catwoman dangerously drawn to each other while suited up, yet painfully unable to relate when freed from their costumes and their masks.

Masks in this country symbolize hiding, but when I used to go to Hallowe'en parties wearing a mask it was actually more of a doorway, a way of expressing myself. There is something about being hidden that in some weird way helps you to be more open because you feel freer. People would open up much more. They were always a little bit wilder, because something about wearing a mask protected them. It's something I have noticed in our culture and have felt myself. When people are covered, a certain weird freedom comes to the surface. It seems that the opposite should be true, but I've found that it isn't.

Some actors have really tapped into the energy of dressing up. I've always loved it on every movie I've ever done. Michael and I used to joke

Michelle Pfeiffer and Tim Burton

about it all the time and sometimes we'd just burst out laughing. You're in this costume and it's like a joke, it's unbelievable, and in some ways it's quite good because you can never take it seriously. There's something beautiful about that.

In one of the film's finest moments, Michael Keaton's Bruce Wayne is dancing with Michelle Pfeiffer's Selina Kyle at a masked ball when they both realize the other's secret identity, and Kyle, who has earlier admitted 'she's sick of masks', asks, 'Does this mean we have to start fighting?'

I think the actors got that very well, because they certainly had been going through it for some time. In some ways it's crazy, because there were so many restrictions with the kind of outfits, make-up and masks they were wearing – it's rather perverse how restricting in a physical sense it often is – that they began to feel that they were not emoting at all, but they were. So, by the time it got to the ball scene I think they could just feel it, it was just there.

Catwoman represents Burton's strongest female character; her relation-

Catwoman and Batman: sick of masks

ship with Keaton's Batman crackles with an intensity that is in marked contrast to that between Keaton and Kim Basinger's clichéd love interest, Vicky Vale, from the first movie.

Some of that is just the unfortunate conventions of movies. I mean, Catwoman is one of my favourite characters, but there is some truth to the criticism that certain characters are not as fleshed out or as wild as some of the others. But those characters are very important too; without the Adam and Barbara characters being kind of boring, Betelgeuse would have had nothing to play off against. Michael got the same criticism in *Batman*, but I always found him to be very compelling and real, which is particularly difficult in a fantastical setting. It's a very underneath the surface kind of service that those characters provide for the movies, and I find them to be more compelling than a lot of people do.

Although Warner Bros had, at great expense, kept the huge Gotham City set up at Pinewood Studios, Burton decided to film on soundstages on the Warners lot in Burbank instead. Bo Welch, Burton's production designer on Beetlejuice *and* Edward Scissorhands, *was employed to supervise the building of a new Gotham City, which retained Anton Furst's hellish feel, but which, according to Welch, was more American than the original's metropolis and contained 'more wit and irony'. Furst, who after* Batman *had been trying to get several directing projects off the ground and had designed Planet Hollywood in New York, was for contractual reasons unable to do the sequel. He committed suicide three months after* Batman Returns *began principal photography in September 1991.*

I decided to do it in LA just because it made more sense to do it there. I think it was felt that it could be kept more secure there, given what happened with the press on the first one. The dollar was probably even worse and it didn't make any sense to do it in England. Also, I wanted to do it in LA because I thought I could use more people that I know from here, actors like Paul Reubens, because to do it over there in England would mean taking some actors, but not all. I was really just looking for a different energy to it. It's closer to *Beetlejuice* in some ways than it is to the other *Batman.* There's a weirder energy to it than the first; the first *Batman* is, I think, a little more controlled. But I didn't think about that, I just tried to treat it like a regular movie and do the things that I wanted to see, which again, I realize, on something like this is a little dangerous. People would pick on certain things, like: 'What's that black stuff coming out of The Penguin's mouth?' I would say to them, 'I don't know, but I can send it in and have it analysed. He's filled with bile, he's a dark little character and he got a lot of things inside him, but I can get a chemical breakdown if you like.' It's good for me to be questioned about certain things; I think it's healthy for me not just to spin off into the cosmos, but people do it to ridiculous extremes.

Everything happens randomly on the set because there are so many things that can go wrong. I've probably been derailed more in terms of things that I've planned than those that I haven't, because so many things can go wrong. So I try in meetings with actors and everybody who is working on the film – costume designer, production designer – to make sure that everybody is on the same wavelength to some degree. So that when you get on the set it's like: here are all the realities of this day, of these people, of what we have, of what we don't have, the weather, the conditions, so let's try to make the best of it. And then, just hope. I don't do a lot of rehearsing. I get in there and block the scene and feel it out with people in their costumes and stuff, because everything suggests something and it's really hard to lock in, one hundred per cent, to what that is until all the elements are there together. So it gets to be much more of a last minute thing.

I would say I shoot an average of maybe five or six takes. That's if everything is okay technically. Often, I shoot more when there are technical problems or special effects involved. Usually I take it as it comes when I get on set. Sometimes if I do a little sketch, it will suggest a shot and I'll have something in mind. But usually I just go with it. Again, actors bring something to everything; each actor has their own set of issues, so something will be suggested by how they look in their costume. So, again, it's got to be right then and there on the set.

To transform Danny De Vito into The Penguin, Burton again called upon Stan Winston whose talented team of artists and technicians fashioned The Penguin's grotesque look from a sketch of Burton's. To create The Penguin's bird army, however, a combination of techniques were utilized, including men in suits, computer-generated imagery, robotic creatures and even real penguins.

The Penguin

I don't really like using real animals because they're in an unnatural setting. I love animals, and that's why I could never watch *Lassie*. I couldn't sleep on Sunday nights if I ever watched it because I don't like seeing animals in jeopardy. I worry more about them than I do the actors, or anybody else. I have a real strong sense of standards with that. There's a lot of added stress there I would rather not have. I love animals and I like learning about them and seeing them, but given that we didn't take them from the wild and torture them and stuff, it was okay.

Batman Returns *continued a trend that has followed through all the films Burton has directed, up to and including* Ed Wood, *in that all his*

Danny De Vito

The Penguin's army ...

... in action

films are named after the main character.

That's something I've never thought about, now that you mention it, and I have no real answer for that except that none of them really have a plot. They're all weird little character pieces, I guess, even though nobody would necessarily perceive them as that. I guess I have just been drawn to the names and who they are, even on a kind of symbolic level. Again, I don't think anybody would consider these pictures to be in-depth character studies, but in some ways they're alternative little character pieces.

Batman Returns *opened in America on 19 July 1992 and shattered its predecessor's record for the most successful three-day opening in history with receipts of $47.7 million. The film eventually grossed $268 million worldwide, but was considered by many critics to be 'too dark'.*

In retrospect I don't think Warners were very happy with the movie. That's my feeling. I had put them through a lot, but I was just trying to give them a good movie. The first one was very successful and there are all of those traps that go along with that, but I tried not to think too much about that and just make a good, fun movie. A lot of it was, I think, just the sheer size of the production. They always want you to go faster, they always want you to hurry up. These kind of productions are big; it's not an exact science and I was going through a lot at the time. It probably had more to do with personal things than anything else. There was the death of a friend of mine, I was having trouble in a relationship, and sometimes, consciously, you don't know until later what's wrong. I just thought it was the hellish shoot of this movie, which didn't help the situation at all.

But I really like the film. I like it better than the first one. There was a big backlash that it was too dark, but I found this movie much less dark than the first one. It's just the cultural climate. And they hear that. They listen to that. I guess they have to to some degree. I don't want to because I think it's dangerous and perverse. I think the culture is much more disturbed and disturbing than this movie, a lot more. But they just fixate on things and they choose targets. I like the movie and I don't feel bad about it, and in some ways it's a purer form of what the *Batman* material is all about, which is that the line between villain and hero is blurred. Max Shreck was like the catalyst of all the characters, which I liked. He was the one who wasn't wearing the mask but, in some ways he was. And the film, in some ways, is just a visual comment on the differences in perception of what is good and bad.

Critics of Burton's work have constantly pointed to what they term his inability to tell a coherent story, and with Batman Returns *he was again accused of sacrificing the narrative for the sake of the visuals.*

I guess it must be the way my brain works, because the first *Batman* was probably my most concentrated effort to tell a linear story, and I realize that it's like a joke. I realized from *Beetlejuice* that there are some people who can do that, and that's fine. In any of my movies the narrative is the worst thing you've ever seen, and that's constant. I don't know why people are so into that because there are lots of movies that have a strong narrative, and I love those. But there are other types as well. Do Fellini movies have a strong narrative drive? I love movies where I make up my own idea about them. In fact, there'll be movies that maybe aren't even about what I think they're about. I just like making things up. Everybody is different, so things are going to affect people differently. So why not have your own opinions, have different levels of things you can find if you want them, however deeply you want to go. That's why I like Roman Polanski's movies, like *The Tenant*. I've felt like that, I've lived it, I know what that's like. Or *Repulsion*, I know that feeling, I understand it. *Bitter Moon*, I've seen that happen. You just connect. It may not be something that anybody else connects with, but it's like *I* get that, *I* understand that feeling. I will always fight that literal impulse to lay everything directly in front of you. I just hate it.

Some people are really good at narrative and some people are really good at action. I'm not that sort of person. So, if I'm going to do something, just let me do my thing and hope for the best. If you don't want me to do it, then don't have me do it. But if I do it, then don't make me conform. If you want it to be a James Cameron movie then get James Cameron to do it. Me directing action is a joke; I don't like guns. I hear a gunshot and I close my eyes. But again it comes down to your interpretation of action. I mean, there's plenty of action in a *Godzilla* movie, but I don't know if people would consider that action.

The Nightmare Before Christmas

After completing Vincent *in 1982, Burton had begun work on another project based on a poem he had written, this time inspired by Clement Clarke Moore's* The Night Before Christmas. *Entitled* The Nightmare Before Christmas, *it told the story of the misguided passion of Jack Skellington, the Pumpkin King of Hallowe'entown, who stumbles upon a door to Christmastown, and is so taken by what he sees that he returns home obsessed with bringing Christmas under his control.*

The initial impulse for doing it was the love of Dr Seuss and those holiday specials that I grew up watching, like *How the Grinch Stole Christmas* and *Rudolph the Red-Nosed Reindeer*. Those crude stop-motion animation holiday things that were on year in, year out make an impact on you early and stay with you. I had grown up with those and had a real feeling for them, and I think, without being too direct, the impulse was to do something like that.

When I first wrote the poem I had Vincent Price in mind as the narrator. He was the overall inspiration for the project because initially I was going to do it with him narrating, like a more expanded version of *Vincent*. Back then I think I would have done it as anything – a television special, a short film – whatever would have gotten it done at the time. It was a funny project because everybody was really nice about it, but it was like being in that show *The Prisoner*; everybody's really nice, but you know you're never going to get out, it's not going to happen. I took it around the networks, did storyboards and sketches and Rick Heinrichs did a little model of Jack. Everybody said they liked it, but not enough to do it at that time. I guess that was my first real taste of that kind of show-business mentality – a nice big smile and an 'Oh yeah, we're going to do this'. But, as you proceed, it becomes less and less of a reality.

It was after *Vincent*, so I was really into stop-motion. I'd seen clay-mation, I'd seen stop-motion, the Harryhausen things. On *Vincent* we weren't trying to push the boundaries of great animation. What we were trying to do with it in a very simple way was be more specific with the design. To me, in claymation the design elements get lost. So what we wanted to do was what you do in a drawing, but just spring it to the third dimension. I always thought that *Nightmare* should be done better than *Vincent*, but at the time I was just thinking of that simple, emotional, trying to make it a well-designed type of animation. I think it's harder to do emotional stuff in three dimensions. In so many ways drawn animation is easier because you can truly do anything, you can draw *anything*. Three-dimensional animation has limitations because you're moving puppets around. But I think when it works it is more effective because it is three-dimensional, and it feels like it's *there*.

The characters that were designed for *Nightmare* had the added burden of not having any eyeballs. The first rule of animation is: Eyes for Expression. But a lot of the characters either don't have any eyes, or their eyes are sewn shut. I thought if we could give life to these characters that have no eyes, it would be great. So, after drawing all those foxes with their wet drippy eyes at Disney, there was a little subversion in having these characters with no eyes. It was funny to think of a character that had these big black holes and to try and make that work.

The idea behind *Nightmare* also came from a combination of feelings to do with love for those *Rudolph* things. Thematically that's something that I like, still respond to, and have responded to in other films about that type of character, somebody, like a Grinch, who is perceived as scary but isn't. Again, that goes back to the monster movies I liked as a kid. They were perceived as frightening and bad, but they're weren't. It's also true in society; people get perceived that way all the time. I felt that way and I never liked it, therefore I always liked characters who were passionate and felt certain ways, but weren't what they were perceived to be. Jack is like a lot of characters in classic literature that are passionate and have a desire to do something in a way that isn't really acknowledged, just like that Don Quixote story, in which some character is on a quest for some sort of feeling, not even knowing what that is. It's a very primal thing to me, that kind of searching for something and not even knowing what it is, but being passionate about it. There are just aspects to the character of Jack that I like and identify with. It means something to me.

When I developed it originally, it was during the period when Disney was actually changing over, and when I didn't know if I was still an employee or not. I was just hanging around. I always felt that it was one project that I would like to make, I felt so secure about it. There was talk of doing it as a kind of TV special, or doing it drawn. But I just didn't want to do any of that. So, I decided to bury it, but always with that feel-

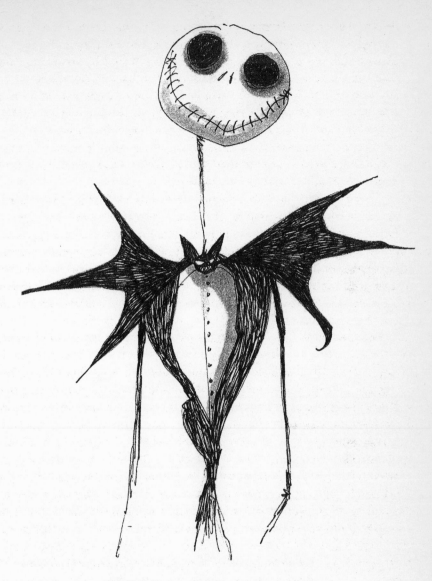

Jack Skellington: big black holes for eyes

ing that I would do it some time. It was weird, some projects you feel more like, 'Oh, I'd better do this now or never', but I never felt that way about *Nightmare*.

Over the years Burton's thoughts regularly returned to the project and in

1990 he had his agent check to see whether Disney still owned the rights to Nightmare *with a view to resurrecting it.*

I didn't even know if they owned it. So we tried to quietly say, 'Can we look around your basement?' And they did own it, because they own everything. There's this thing you sign when you work there, which states that any thoughts you have during your employment are owned by the thought police. Obviously, there's no real way of doing it quietly. We tried, but they were soon right there and they were fine – which is against their nature – so I'm very respectful and feel honoured that they let it happen. This was after *Edward Scissorhands* and *Batman,* and the reason it got made is because I've been lucky enough to be successful. That's really the only reason it got made. It certainly wasn't a case of the time being right. But I will say this about Disney, they at least understood our trying to push the envelope a little bit as far as the animation was concerned, they were responsive to that.

Recognizing the treasure locked in their vaults, Disney immediately leapt at the chance to work with Burton, and saw in his desire to produce a full-length stop-motion animated feature a way of further enhancing their reputation in animation. Though stop-motion had first been seen in 1907 in J. Stuart Blackton's The Haunted Hotel, *it was Willis O'Brien who pioneered stop-motion as an effects technique in 1925 in* The Lost World *and then, most memorably, in creating* King Kong *in 1933. He passed his mantle to Ray Harryhausen, who in turn created a coterie of fantastical creatures for films such as* Jason and the Argonauts *and the* Sinbad *series. The introduction of go-motion – a variation on stop-motion in which objects are blurred in the frame to produce a more realistic effect – in 1983 by Industrial Light and Magic for* Return of the Jedi, *and the advancement in computer-generated imagery, meant effects that would have previously been the domain of stop-motion could now be created by computer. This contributed to stop-motion's cinematic decline, though animators such as Nick Park in England, creator of the Oscar-winning* Creature Comforts, *and Henry Selick in the United States, with his commercials, idents for MTV and short films, kept the art very much alive and kicking.*

It's a funky old art form stop-motion, and even though new technology was used at times in *Nightmare,* basically it's artists doing it and painting sets and making things. There's something very gratifying about that, something I love and never want to forget. It's the handmade aspect of things, part of an energy that you can't explain. You can sense it when you see the concentration of the animators as they move the figures, there's an energy that's captured. It's like when you look at a Van Gogh painting. I remember the first time I saw one in reality. You've seen them in books, but the energy that's captured on the canvas is incredible, and I think that's something that nobody talks about because it's not something literal.

It's the same with this kind of animation, and I think that's the power of Ray Harryhausen. When it's done beautifully, you feel somebody's energy. It's something that computers will never be able to replace, because they're missing that one element. For as good as computers are and as incredible as it will get and is right now, it goes back to painters and their canvases. This project and these characters and these visuals, the only way that it could have been done was with stop-motion. Therefore, it's very specialized. I remember getting shots and each time I would see a shot I would get this little rush of energy; it was so beautiful. It's like a drug. And I realized if you did it in live-action it wouldn't be as good; if you did it in drawing it wouldn't be as good. There is something about stop-motion that gives it an energy that you don't get in any other form.

Despite Nightmare's *proximity to his heart, Burton passed on directing the project because of his commitment to* Batman Returns *and the painstakingly slow production period necessary to complete a project of this kind. Instead, he chose Henry Selick, whom he had first met at Disney in the late seventies and to whom he had shown his original* Nightmare *sketches in 1982. Since the early eighties, Selick had been living and working in San Francisco, an area that had become the centre for stop-motion animators. It was here that Disney's adult-orientated arm Touchstone Pictures and Burton set up Skellington Productions, and began work on* Nightmare *in July 1991.*

Henry is a real artist. He's truly the best. He had done a lot of great stuff for MTV and was doing a lot of great stuff for stop-motion animation. There was a whole group of really talented artists up there in San Francisco. It's just that, even more than with drawn animation, it's hard to find people who are really talented at it, because it's a much more rarified form, and such an intense process. So, they let us do it up in San Francisco.

When I wasn't shooting I would go up there because I loved it, but most of the time Henry would just send me stuff – there'd be a few shots during the week – and so over the period of a couple of years it all came together. I'm trying to think when it started, but I am the worst person when it comes dates. Have you noticed that? I just have the worst mind when it comes to that. Everything is true, it's just that the time frame is a little off-kilter. Anyway, I would get a reel and I had an editing room and I would edit some shots when I was working on the second *Batman* movie. At that stage, there's something about it taking so long that means you can just sit there and enjoy it, and look at the texture.

It was the hardest thing I ever worked on, in a way, because it just took so long, and there were a lot of people involved, a lot of artists. Hopefully, most people you work with are artists, but it's an intense thing, stop-motion animation, and the thing that I was looking for all the time was just the feeling of it. Everybody contributed something, everybody had ideas and stuff, but what I always tried to do was just go back to that initial feeling. And even though it expanded, I would try to keep it on a certain track. It's funny, because when a project takes that much time, and I've been in animation so I know, ideas come all the time. That's fine, but sometimes the ideas are scary because people want to change this and change that. That's just the nature of it, because the ideas are quicker than the process. So, I tried to keep a constant watch. Actually, I enjoyed working in this way because the project took three years, and even if I was working on other things I could make a sketch or comment on things. And as the shots got assembled, I just tried to run it through that original feeling.

I guess my main concern, was that Henry, being an artist in his own right, wouldn't do the things I wanted. I was worried about that kind of tension. But it wasn't like that. He was great. That's why it's important very early on for people to be in synch about a project. So those early meetings are almost the most important. It's like, if you were doing a book, you would try to be faithful to the material. I wanted to feel comfortable that Henry was into that, otherwise you'd be fighting all time, and that couldn't happen. I've known some people who like to fight, who like that kind of struggle on set. I don't really like that. I don't like working with actors who aren't into it. You want people that are one hundred per cent into a project, even if they don't completely get it. So, there was no better group of people to do that movie and I always felt it was a special time. The studio was incredible and I just loved going up there because that level of artistry and detail was magical, truly magical and I'd never really felt that before.

To adapt his original, three-page poem into a feature-length script, Burton originally called upon Beetlejuice *writer Michael McDowell. But when the collaboration didn't pan out quite the way Burton planned, he decided to attack the project from a musical standpoint and turned to his regular partner Danny Elfman. Together, Burton and Elfman, who also provides the singing voice of Jack in the movie, fleshed out a rough storyline and two-thirds of the film's songs, which Selick and his team of animators began work on even before Caroline Thompson was brought in to incorporate them into a screenplay.*

I brought Michael in at the beginning and I realized that the way I really should do it was the way Danny and I eventually did it, even though it's not the most logical way. Michael's a friend, but it just didn't work. What Danny and I had when we started was the poem that I wrote and some drawings and some storyboards, and also this story outline I did about ten years ago. I would go over to his house and we would just treat it like an operetta, not like the musicals that they did, but more like that old-fashioned kind of thing, where the songs are more engrained in the story. I would begin to tell him the story and he'd write a song; he wrote them pretty quickly, actually, at least the initial pass on them. We worked in a weird way, where there was the outline and the songs and then we worked out the script. There was a lot going on, that was what was so difficult about it. They were doing the storyboards up there, we were doing the script, all this stuff was happening at once. It's not the best way to do it, but this was a new thing we were trying to do. I had seen other stop-motion animated features, and they were either not engaging or they're just too bizarre. There was one I liked when I was a kid called *Mad Monster Party*. People thought *Nightmare* was the first stop-motion animated monster musical, but that was.

So, Danny and I would go through my little outline and I'd say Jack does this and then he does that and then he falls into Christmastown. We'd worked together so much that it didn't matter that we didn't know what we were doing; at least we knew each other. So we just took at stab at it. And again, since we had worked together before, he worked very quickly, which was good because we needed the songs so we could do the script. He wrote them fairly quickly, within a couple of months; he would play me stuff the next week, sometimes the next day. Then I brought in Caroline and she knew Danny. It was a gradual, evolving process: there's Henry, there's me, there's Danny, there's Caroline, and that's a lot to deal with. And then you add in the other incredible artists.

The Nightmare Before Christmas: sketches

While Burton and Elfman had no specific style in mind for the film's musical numbers, preferring to see where the story took them, the one sung by Oogie Boogie Man was patterned after a character found in Max Fleischer's Betty Boop cartoons, which was voiced by Cab Calloway.

I remember drawing Jack and really getting into these black holes for eyes and thinking that to be expressive, but not have any eyes, would be really incredible. Sally was a relatively new character; I was into stitching from

The Nightmare Before Christmas: Sally and Jack

the Catwoman thing, I was into that whole psychological thing of being pieced together. Again, these are all symbols for the way that you feel. The feeling of not being together and of being loosely stitched together and constantly trying to pull yourself together, so to speak, is just a strong feeling to me. So those kind of visual symbols have less to do with being based on *Frankenstein*, than with the feeling of pulling yourself together.

The Cab Calloway thing was a more specific reference, however; when Danny and I were talking about it, it had more to do with this feeling of remembering, because I remember seeing these Betty Boop cartoons, where this weird character would come out. I didn't know who it was, but it would do this weird musical number in the middle of nowhere, and it was like: 'What the hell is that?' Again, it had to do with a feeling of remembering that from when I was a child. A lot of those images come more from feelings than they do from anything specific.

It's funny, because of the movies I've done, a lot of people think that they're very much about the way they look. People don't realize that everything I've ever done has to mean something; even if it's not clear-cut to anybody else, I have to find some connection, and actually the more absurd the element, the more I have to feel that I understand something behind it. That's why we're all fascinated by the movies. They tap into your dreams and your subconscious. I guess it is different from generation to generation, but movies are truly a form of therapy and work on your subconscious in the way fairy tales were meant to. The Dog Woman and Lizard Man in those Indian tales, they're not meant to be taken literally. That's what movies do as well. I was never a scholar in any of that stuff, but I always appreciated it. It's something I've found is not ingrained in American culture, that sense of myth or folklore. The best America could do is Johnny Appleseed – kind of soft, mutated.

The Nightmare Before Christmas *marked Burton's third movie in a row to be set at Christmas.*

I think I'm off that for a while. I've exorcized my Christmas demons. Growing up in Burbank, I responded to the holidays, especially Hallowe'en and Christmas, because they were the most visual and fun in some respects. The best I can decipher from the whole thing is that when you grow up in a blank environment, any form of ritual, like a holiday, gives you a sense of place. Most other countries are rich with ritual, but I guess America is a relatively new country and a fairly Puritan one. Growing up in a suburban environment where it's pushed even further in that direction, makes you feel very floaty. So holidays, especially those two, were very much a grounding or a way to experience seasons, because in California you don't get any. So at least you could walk in the supermarket aisles and see the Hallowe'en display and the fall leaves, because you certainly couldn't experience it in the weather and the environment.

To me, Hallowe'en has always been the most fun night of the year. It's where rules are dropped and you can be anything at all. Fantasy rules. It's only scary in a funny way. Nobody's out to really scare anybody else to death. They're out to delight people with their scariness, which is what Hallowe'en is all about and what *Nightmare* is all about.

'I've exorized my Christmas demons'

The budget for Nightmare *was less than $18 million, a fraction of the cost of producing a drawn animated movie. The film was released on Hallowe'en 1993 in the US and made $51 million at the box office. Rather ironically, it was (mis)perceived as being too scary for kids.*

Which was great, which was interesting, because it's what the story is about. Here you have this story where there are no really bad characters, not even Oogie Boogie; he's not *really* bad, he's just the weird neighbour in this weird city. And you have this character, Jack, who just wants to do good; he's passionate about something, and basically he ends up being misperceived and scaring everybody. It's funny, it took on the life of what it was about in real life. It was like, 'Wait a minute. This is *exactly* what the movie is about. People are freaking out because they think it's scary, but it's not. There really isn't anything in it.' Kids are incredible. If you show it to a bunch of kids without their parents it's great, but as soon as you get the parents involved, you get: 'This is too scary.' I've seen this happen before and it's a very disturbing phenomenon. If something was too scary for me, I wouldn't watch it, I was never forced to, but when you get a parent giving you this weird vibe, it puts you on edge.

It was released as *Tim Burton's The Nightmare Before Christmas*

'Hallowe'en has always been the most fun night of the year'

because they felt it would help. But it turned into more of a brand-name thing, it turned into something else, which I'm not quite sure about. Initially, they had talked to me about what that would achieve; smaller print above the title would give it a certain kind of context which they felt would help the movie, and I went along with it. I wouldn't do that with everything. There are only a few projects that you feel so personally involved with. I felt that way about *Vincent*, and I felt that way about this. But you don't really have any control over what happens outside. I learned that on the first *Batman*, where what you read about and what actually happened were two different things.

Sometimes I'll see people wearing the *Nightmare* Burger King watch in the weirdest places. I just saw somebody wearing it who worked at Carnegie Hall, and it's incredible. People will come up and they'll have a little picture of Jack with them. It's funny because sometimes when things connect with people, maybe not a large group, but with some, it's really wonderful to me. A lot of people and critics don't get that there is an emotion underneath these weird, stupid-looking things. Some people do, and that probably means the most to me: that people get the emotional quality underneath the stupid façade.

Because of the sheer scale and length of the project, which encompassed the period he was directing Batman Returns, The Nightmare Before Christmas *represented the first time that Burton had worked on more than one film at a time.*

That was the first time where there was a lot of energy put into a couple of different things, *Batman Returns* and *Nightmare*. It was kind of heavy. I can only work on one thing at a time, unless I find the right people. A lot of it has to do with finding kindred spirits, so to speak; it really does do a lot for you, you work on a higher level that way. I find if somebody isn't going with the flow, it's not the best working relationship anyway, so it's nice to work with people who are on the same wavelength. Then they surprise you and there's less stress and it's more creative. It's better.

I have to give credit to the people in charge at Disney now because they have certainly made the place more successful; they have more of an idea about what's going on. When I was there, there was a group of people who could have done *The Little Mermaid,* and things like that, back then. They had that pool of talent, even stronger, ten, fifteen years ago; they could have ushered in that renaissance back then had they been given the opportunity. At the time most people were out of Cal Arts, or college. Disney was just opening up, hiring young people, and everybody was completely eager to go for it and make a great movie, everybody was a Disneyphile. It's not like they were wanting to bring Disney animation into the R-rated world. So there was that talent, and finally the regime that's there now recognized that talent and have obviously been very successful in bringing the studio around, and that's good for animation as a whole.

Cabin Boy and *Ed Wood*

Following The Nightmare Before Christmas, *Burton co-produced, with Denise Di Novi,* Cabin Boy *for Disney. The film, a camp homage to the Sinbad movies starring Chris Elliott, Ricki Lake and Russ Tamblyn, was a massive critical and box-office disaster.*

It was sort of a weird comedy, and I didn't want to direct it because I thought it would be too expensive. But it didn't meet with too much critical or financial approval. Disney didn't like it; they didn't get it, and it just fell by the wayside. It was directed by Adam Resnick, who wrote it with some people who were on *The David Letterman Show*. I just tried to pass on my expertise on certain things, but I couldn't be there all the time, and I think I've learned a bit of a lesson from that. It's like on *Nightmare*, I was working on something else, but that project was different because I loved that one, it was my thing. But with *Cabin Boy*, I didn't know what was going on. I think I've just got to get involved with something or not do it. I don't think I would do anything like that again, not unless I felt the same way as I did about *Nightmare*. People ask me, but I won't unless I feel very confident about certain things.

Burton was set to direct Mary Reilly, *for Columbia Pictures, a version of Robert Louis Stevenson's oft-filmed tale* Dr Jekyll and Mr Hyde, *told this time from the point of view of Jekyll's housekeeper, with* Beetlejuice *and* Edward Scissorhands *star Winona Ryder in the title role.*

I was into that for a while, but what happened was the studio wanted to push it. Whereas before I could take my time to decide about things, in Hollywood you get shoved into this whole commercial thing. They want the movie. I remember them coming up to me and going, 'Oh, we've got five different directors who want to do this movie.' And I remember being turned off by the process. It's like, 'Well, you know, if you've got five other people that want to do it, maybe you should have them do it.' So basically they speeded me out of the project, because they saw it in a certain way. They saw it with Julia Roberts, and now they're getting what they want. I don't know what they think. I think they've got a weird feeling about me. I don't follow their way of thinking a lot of the time.

He was replaced on Mary Reilly *by Stephen Frears, and Julia Roberts was indeed cast in the title role opposite John Malkovich. Meanwhile Burton had become interested in a project based on the life of Edward D. Wood Jr that had been brought to his attention by Larry Karaszewski and Scott Alexander, the writers of the* Problem Child *movies. Karaszewski and Alexander had toyed with the idea of writing a film about Wood, often referred to as the world's worst director, ever since they were students at the University of Southern California film school. Irritated at being thought of solely as writers of kids' movies, they wrote a ten-page treatment and pitched the idea to* Heathers' *director Michael Lehman, with whom they were at USC. He, in turn, took the project to his producer on* Heathers, *Denise Di Novi. A deal was struck with Lehman as director and Burton and Di Novi producing. When* Mary Reilly *fell through, Burton became interested in directing* Ed Wood *himself, on the understanding that it could be done quickly. With this in mind Karaszewski and Alexander delivered a 147-page screenplay in six weeks. Burton read the first draft and immediately agreed to direct it as it stood, without any changes or rewrites.*

Wood, the director of such cult classics as Glen or Glenda, Bride of the Monster *and, most infamously,* Plan 9 From Outer Space, *died in 1978, aged fifty-four, penniless and forgotten. Sadly he achieved near legendary status only posthumously, in the early eighties, thanks to publications such as Michael and Harry Medveds'* The Golden Turkey Awards, *which voted* Plan 9 *the worst film of all time. Born in Poughkeepsie, New York in 1924, Wood lived his entire life on the cusp of Hollywood, aspiring to be the next Orson Welles, but never even coming remotely close. A famed transvestite with a fondness for angora sweaters and an engaging personality, Wood surrounded himself with a bizarre coterie of admirers and wannabes, including Criswell, a showman/psychic, Tor Johnson, a Swedish wrestler, and Vampira, a TV horror show host, many of whom believed Ed was going to make them stars. In 1953, Wood met his idol Bela Lugosi, a Hungarian immigrant and the celebrated star of Universal's 1930 version of* Dracula. *In the two decades since the release of* Dracula, *Lugosi had slipped into virtual anonymity and become addict-*

ed to morphine, which he had been prescribed to relieve the pain from a war wound. Wood vowed to revitalize his career by putting him in his movies, giving him roles in both Glen or Glenda, *Wood's autobiographical tale of a transvestite (played by Wood under the name of Daniel Davis) and* Bride of the Monster, *and using the last remaining footage he shot of Lugosi as the basis for* Plan 9. *Karaszewski and Alexander's script follows Wood's life through these three movies, and focuses on the Wood/Lugosi relationship, one that both they and Burton acknowledge is not unlike the friendship between Burton and his idol, Vincent Price.*

Denise had talked about producing this movie that Larry and Scott wanted to write. I was in Poughkeepsie, in upstate New York at the time. It was after *Batman Returns* when I was working on the *Nightmare* book, and I didn't know what I wanted to do. I started thinking about the idea of *Ed Wood*, and I started making notes and stuff because I was going to produce it. And then I thought, 'You know what, I like these people, and I want to direct it.' What was odd was that Ed Wood was from Poughkeepsie, which is where I was hanging around, and I had thought, 'This is cool, this is a weird place.' I got a kind of karmic rush when I decided to do it, and then I read this book *Nightmare of Ecstasy* and realized Ed Wood was from Poughkeepsie. So there was this weird connection and I just started to get into it. I talked to Scott and Larry and they wrote a script really quickly, within a month. I've never seen a script get written so fast and it was really long too, like 150 pages. They certainly had it in them, those guys. They were fans. They were into it. I just started doing what I usually do, which is to look for the emotional connections.

There were aspects of the character and his thing with Bela Lugosi that I immediately responded to. What's great about *Ed Wood* is that it's rough, it's not like a completely hardcore realistic biopic. In doing a biopic you can't help but get inside the person's spirit a little bit, so for me, some of the film is trying to be through Ed a little bit. So it's got an overly optimistic quality to it.

I grew up loving *Plan 9*, which is a movie you see when you're a kid and it remains with you. And then later on, Wood gets acknowledged as the worst director in the world, and then starts to get a little bit more known, and then there are festivals, and they show his movies and everybody laughs at them. But the thing is, when you watch his movies, yeah, they are bad, but they're special. There's some reason why these movies remain there, and are acknowledged, beyond the fact that they're purely bad. There's a certain consistency to them, and a certain kind of weird artistry. I mean, they are unlike any other thing. He didn't let technicalities like visible wires and bad sets distract him from his story-telling. There's a twisted form of integrity to that.

Ed Wood is very much the classic Burton character: a misfit, a misunderstood, misperceived individual.

He fits that theme, yes, but I think the difference with Ed, unlike the other characters, is that there are some different elements to him. What I liked about Ed Wood is that he is so optimistic. The thing I was taken by back when I'd read interviews with Ed Wood, especially since I knew the movies and the other aspects of his life, was his extreme optimism, to the point where there was an incredible amount of denial. And there's something charming to me about that. It's like with the Catwoman or the Sally characters – the idea of pulling themselves together, the stitching. Being passionate and optimistic is great to a certain point, and then you're just in complete denial, it becomes delusional. That's what I liked about the Ed Wood character. I could relate to him that way. I think everybody is in some form of denial. Denial is an incredible thing. Most people don't go through life with an extreme awareness of every aspect of themselves.

People think it's funny that I did this movie. Because I've been so successful, why would I want to make a movie about somebody who's not successful? But the way I feel about that, and him and me, is that any of my movies could go either way, they really could, and so the line between success and failure is a very thin one. That's why I responded so much to him. I believe that and, who knows, I could become Ed Wood tomorrow. Believe me, if you asked the studio before any of the movies that I've worked on have come out, they wouldn't have predicted their success. If it's a movie like *Lethal Weapon,* then they feel more comfortable. They know it's probably going to be okay. But the films that I've worked on, there's never been that certainty or feeling of confidence. And so I respond to Ed. I love him because he's got enthusiasm, and he's flawed, and there's that delusional sort of feeling.

And there was an aspect of his relationship with Bela Lugosi that I liked. He befriended him at the end of his life, and without really knowing what that was like, I connected with it on the level that I did with Vincent Price, in terms of how I felt about him. Meeting Vincent had an incredible impact on me, the same impact Ed must have felt meeting and working

Tim Burton directing *Ed Wood*

'I love Ed because he's got enthusiasm.' (Johnny Depp as Ed Wood)

Bela (Martin Landau) and Ed (Johnny Depp): 'There was an aspect of Ed's relationship with Bela Lugosi that I liked.'

'There's something very appealing about people that go out on a limb.' (Jeffrey Jones, Sarah Jessica Parker, Martin Landau, Johnny Depp, George 'The Animal' Steele, Max Casella and Brent Hinkley)

with his idol. And then there was this weird group of people that hung around with Ed. I liked the people. I just liked the idea of them. I liked that they were all completely out of it and everybody thought they were doing the greatest things, but they weren't. There's something that's very appealing about people who go out on a limb, who are perceived by society to be something else. In some ways, that loosens them up just to be themselves.

There are similarities between myself and Ed. Whether or not people sense it, I always try to relate to all those characters. There are aspects of Ed Wood that I can identify with because I think you have to, because, as I said, I'm not proficient enough to wing it. It's like, even if nobody else understands it, even if the movie comes out and everybody goes, 'What the hell is this?', for me to do it I have to relate to him. I have to be on his journey with him.

One of the things I liked about Ed, and I could relate to, was being passionate about what you do to the point of it becoming like a weird drug. It's like with any movie I've ever made, you get caught up in it; you're there and you think you are doing the greatest thing in the world. You have to think that. But you thinking you're doing the greatest thing in the world maybe doesn't have anything to do with how the rest of the population perceives it. So yes, I definitely felt and feel that way. Again, that's why I admire Ed so much, and those people – he was doing *something*.

If I see something, a piece of work, a painting, a film, anything, and somebody's going out on a limb and doing it, I admire them. I don't even care if I like it, I just admire them, because they're doing something that a lot of people won't do. You meet these people who build weird sculptures out of cars in the desert. I mean, you have to admire those people more than anybody.

I remember around the time I did *Hansel and Gretel* having this feeling that there were a lot of people judging it, and saying this doesn't work, this is bad. And I'm saying to myself, 'Fuck you! You do something. You may be right, but just do something for God's sake!' I like it when people do things. But now there's a lot of people waiting in the wings, there just seems to be more media around, therefore there's more judgement, and more people *not* doing things. The world seems to be getting a lot more judgers and a lot less doers. I've always hated that. That's why *Ed Wood* has a weird tone, because Ed just goes through the movie and remains optimistic.

The film ends with him very optimistic, driving off thinking that he's made, with *Plan 9*, the greatest movie ever. In reality, his story only gets more tragic as it goes along. His life is so bad, it's so redundant, it just gets more and more negative; but we just let him be him, and it ends at that point.

All Burton's characters have a duality to them and Ed's is ostensibly his transvestism.

It's brought out. I try to be matter-of-fact about it. I don't make judgements about people, especially people who I like and don't really know. So it's there, and it's just a part of his life. The thing about transvestism in movies that I've never liked is that it's an easy joke, and I don't know why. I don't like that, so I didn't want to make it a big joke. It's just a part of his life. Some of it's funny, I think. He was a heterosexual who liked to do that. I understand it too, women's clothes *are* more comfortable. If you walk into a clothing shop the women's clothes are the best. Guys' clothes have been the same for years. But they always use the best fabrics for women's clothes. So it's not hard to understand transvestism. But that was a part of his life, and the great thing was that the people around him, for the most part, just accepted it.

There's a moment in the movie which I love, and it's not a big deal, it's something I always liked from the script. It's where he tells his wife, Kathy, and she just accepts it, without any big fanfare. It's just a simple little moment, but that's kind of a fantasy to me. I think why it chokes me up is that it's simple acceptance, which is something you rarely get in life. People rarely accept you for who you are, and when that happens, even on a simple level, it's kind of great.

One can look at Burton's films as being essentially live-action animated movies. Ed Wood, *on the other hand, is a first in that it's a film about people who really existed.*

It is a bit of a departure in that respect, yes. It's real people, but I always treat everybody like real people, it's part of the process for me. I have to believe everybody. These are real people, but the great thing about these real people is that they're real people in *my* sense of real people – which is that they're not. If you read *Nightmare of Ecstasy*, the great thing about these people's story is that there is no story. The book is a series of recollections from these people who have a vague remembrance of this time.

Somebody will say this, somebody will say that, some of it's even contradictory, which I felt is very much in the spirit of this character, but these people, these slightly delusional kind of achievers, have a kind of upbeat 'Let's put on a show' attitude. I always saw it as a weird Andy Hardy movie in a way, because that's what my take on these people was like.

These people were never perceived as real people, they weren't treated seriously. And I guess they were all so out of it that their memories are worse than mine, if you can believe that. So that allowed me the opportunity to take off. You're not dealing with the well-documented life of Orson Welles here. When Ed Wood died he didn't even have an obituary in the paper. He died in this little building on Yucca watching a football game, having a heart attack, and nobody knew who he was.

Initially Ed Wood *was in development with Columbia Pictures, but when Burton decided he wanted to shoot the film in black and white, studio head Mark Canton wouldn't agree to it unless the studio was given a first-look deal. Burton insisted on total control, and so in April 1993, a month before shooting was scheduled to start, Canton put the movie into turnaround. The decision sparked a studio frenzy, with Warners, Paramount and Fox all interested in picking up the option, but Burton decided to accept an offer from Disney, who had previously produced* The Nightmare Before Christmas. *With a budget of $18 million, low by today's standards, Disney didn't feel the movie was that much of a risk, and granted Burton total creative autonomy. He began shooting in August 1993.*

Ed Wood is the hardest movie I've ever had to get off the ground. I thought it would be the easiest movie because I didn't take a fee. I did it for scale, and the fact is it's not that outlandish a movie, either. I mean, believe me, when I read the script I found it to be very good, certainly no weirder than anything else I've done. It's certainly the cheapest movie, cheaper than anything since *Pee-Wee*, and I got most of the actors to do it for not a lot.

The decision to do it in black and white was pretty much the same thought process as with anything you do. We were at make-up artist Rick Baker's with Martin Landau, who plays Bela Lugosi, and we were doing some make-up tests, and we were saying, 'What colour were Bela's eyes?' And then I started thinking, this is bullshit, I don't want to get into this. This should be in black and white because you don't want to be sitting there going, 'What colour were Bela's eyes?' You want to do what's right for the material and the movie, and this was a movie that *had* to be in black and white. Everybody should have the opportunity to say this movie would be better in colour, and then you think about colour. But if it shouldn't be in colour, well then don't make it in colour. It's the same way *Frankenweenie* should be in black and white, *Vincent* should be in black and white, *Beetlejuice* should be in colour, *Pee-Wee's Big Adventure* colour, *Batman* colour. It really should be whatever's best for the movie.

So at some point I had a meeting with Columbia and they just didn't want to go for it. My argument was it doesn't matter if a movie is in black and white or in colour, the movie has to work. I said I can't predict if this movie is going to be successful. I can't predict if any movie is going to be successful. Either it will click with people or it won't, and I'm trying to get it to a place where it has the most potential to click with people, and I feel that this material is black and white. It's not a pretentious thing. In fact, I resist doing things in black and white because I don't want to be perceived as being pretentious. I find that I don't necessarily agree with a lot of things that are done in black and white, but it shouldn't be a big deal. You just make whatever you think is right for the movie. End of story.

Columbia didn't buy it, which is fine, I don't want to be involved with people who don't understand. Who needs it?

I'm in this meeting and they're crowing about their big hit *Last Action Hero*, you know, all egotistical and stuff, and I'm thinking, I'm glad you people know so much. Egotism, that's something I can't tolerate in a field where you don't know shit, nobody knows shit. All you can do is believe in something, care about it and try to make the best movie. I've grown less and less tolerant of all that other bullshit. I'll tolerate a conversation where somebody will say, 'Do you think this is a good idea?' That's legitimate. But it's like living in this complete fantasy world – that's why I'm here in New York, that's why I've gotten out of Hollywood lately, because I don't want to fall into the fantasy world these people create for themselves. The only fantasy world I want to create is in a movie. The fact that people can sit there and spout their philosophy and be egotistical about their big summer hit and think they know what they're talking about is a joke. I was glad that I left.

My leaving opened it up, actually. I did have the relationship with Disney because of *Nightmare*, but I talked to a few people and every other studio besides Columbia was nice about it. They all seemed to get it and want to do it. Certainly it wasn't as big a risk as people thought. Every-

Ed Wood: Sketch for the Spook House

body was a little leery about the black and white, but in the end, and I firmly believe my own philosophy in this case, when I decided to do it in black and white I felt it was the best idea to help the movie be what it should be. Therefore, with that one goal in mind, which is that the movie needs to work, it doesn't matter what colour it is. Disney were the most go-ahead. They're into this thing of changing their image, which I don't think they need to work so hard at.

As with every Burton movie, Ed Wood's *casting is suitably eclectic, with* Edward Scissorhands *star Johnny Depp as Ed, Martin Landau as Lugosi, Bill Murray as Bunny Breckinridge, Ed's transvestite friend, Beetlejuice's Jeffrey Jones as Criswell, Lisa Marie, a former model and now Burton's girlfriend, as Vampira, wrestler George 'The Animal' Steele as Tor Johnson, Sarah Jessica Parker as Ed's girlfriend Deloris and Patricia Arquette as Wood's wife Kathy.*

I tried to get a weird mix of people. Johnny liked the material, he respond-ed to it. I feel close to Johnny because I think somewhere inside we

138

something with skeletons

Ed Wood: Skeleton sketch

respond to similar things, and this was a chance after working on *Edward Scissorhands* to be more open. Edward was interior, this symbol come to life; Ed is more outgoing. It was interesting for me, after working with Johnny before, to explore a more open kind of thing. He did a really great job and he found a tone which I like.

I wanted to go with some knowns and some unknowns, Lisa Marie and George 'The Animal' Steele hadn't acted before; it was like trying to get a mix of people, just like in Ed Wood's movies. I wanted it to have its own kind of weird energy. With Bill Murray I didn't want to get into a situation where it's like a bunch of cameos. But the great thing about Bill in the movie is that he is a character. It's not like: 'Here's Bill Murray.' He plays this weird character that floats in and out. It was important to me to temper it with people who hadn't acted, or maybe hadn't acted as much, just to create an odd mix.

There's something about Martin Landau. I had a feeling about him. He's a man who's been in showbusiness a long time. I don't know what there was about him that made me connect him with the Bela thing, perhaps just talking to him made me feel he was perfect for the part. He's seen a lot, probably like Bela, and been through lots of things. He's cer-

'We re-created a few scenes ...' (George 'The Animal' Steele and Lisa Marie)

tainly not tragic like Bela, but I think he has been in Hollywood long enough to understand those aspects of it. I think he could just relate to it, and had been through enough ups and downs to understand Bela Lugosi. He's got his own presence in his own right. He's done the road tour of *Dracula*. He's been in horror movies. It was a case of 'That guy looks weird, let's put him in a horror movie.' He's been through it. He's worked with Alfred Hitchcock. He's been in cheesy horror movies. It was something he could bring, that knowledge.

As Ed Wood's wife, Kathy, I wanted somebody with presence, because it's not a big role; she comes into it late. Patricia Arquette's got a gravity that I like, and that's what Kathy needed. Those things are the hardest to pull off: simply being there. You just have to have it; it's not something you can create from an outside source, so I was very happy that she did it, because this movie is a hotchpotch of things. It needs the gravity that certain people bring to it.

The funny thing about these people is that none of their lives were really documented. And I know how that feels. These people were a little out of it, they just weren't there. So, now that Ed Wood has come out of the closet, so to speak, and more has been talked about the movies and they have more festivals on him, there's all of this revisionist history. I've seen it happen in my lifetime. It's scary. I got the worst reviews on *Pee-Wee's*

'... but it was more about the shooting of them.'
(Johnny Depp and Norman Alden)

Big Adventure, and then, as the years went by, I would read things from critics saying what a great movie it is. That's why this movie does not pretend that in 1952 Ed Wood actually did this. It's not that. In some ways it's a little subjective, it's an acknowledgement that there is no hard core. I'm only taking what I think some of this stuff is, and trying to project a certain kind of spirit. The movie is dramatic, and I think there are some funny things in it, but it's treading a fine line because I never wanted it to be jokey. Never. I'm *with* them. I'm not laughing at them. I don't quite know how people will perceive the perspective and the energy that that creates because they may go, 'This isn't real.' But you know what, I hate most biopics. I find that most biopics are stodgy and really boring, because people, in my opinion, take too much of a reverential approach and it's fake.

Everytime I've seen a biopic, it just doesn't feel real. There's something about it, the sheer fact that it's a movie and that an actor is portraying someone, means there's a level of façade and fakery to it. I decided to go along with that a little bit more and not to treat these people so reverentially or in a documentary style. In some ways I'm a purist. I wasn't there with these people, I don't know them, but I have a feeling about them. So that's what I'm doing. I'm doing my feeling. I'm sure these people were more horrible than the way I'm portraying them. But these people should feel good, because they've been made fun of their whole lives and I'm certainly not doing that to them. I like them. I did as much research as I could in terms of learning what I wanted to learn about them, but again, the film is just more my idea about these people.

Kathy is still alive. She's very sweet. She loved Ed. That's the other thing, it's nice when people love each other. That's what I loved about her. She loved him, it seems.

Again Burton refrained from going back and reviewing Wood's movies, preferring mainly to go with his memory and his feelings.

We had them around. People watched them. I didn't too much. There might have been certain instances, but again I kind of watched from around a corner. I didn't want to get into too many weird re-creations. I thought, I don't want to sit here and make judgements. I treated it matter-of-factly, so we re-create some stuff, some stuff we don't. We re-created a few scenes from three of the films, but it was more about the shooting of them, the process. It has a fragmented, kind of slightly out of it tone I felt the book had. I had the art department and the people on the movie who hadn't heard of Ed Wood look at the films. I gave them copies of the movies and that Jonathan Ross documentary about Ed. I liked that documentary most because I felt it captured the true spirit of these people.

There's a sparseness to the movie. Again, I don't know how it will come across because it's an amalgam of feelings, and I don't know how they will all finally connect. But the thing I always loved about those Ed Wood movies was that they were relatively timeless. They seemed like they were ahead of their time and behind their time. There was a kind of ponderous sparseness to them that I remember. So a lot of the time I would just try to keep it sparse because that's just the way I felt about them. They were living in their own world.

Surprisingly, given his six-film relationship with Danny Elfman, Burton chose composer Howard Shore to provide the music for Ed Wood.

The situation with Danny right now, I don't know if it will stay that way or not. I don't know what to say about it because I don't know where it's going. We're taking a little vacation from each other.

Ed Wood opened in America on 7 October 1994 to unanimously rave reviews. Burton is producer of the third Batman movie, Batman Forever, *directed by Joel Schumacher.*

I don't think Warners wanted me to direct a third *Batman*. I even said that to them. I think what happened was I went through a lot on the last one; a lot of it was personal, a lot of it had to do with the movie, a lot of it was a desire to make the movie something different. I've always been a little at odds with them. Any time people start saying things are too dark to me I just don't get it, because I have a different perception of what dark is. To me something like *Lethal Weapon* is really dark, whereas to them it's not. They see people walking around in regular clothes shooting guns, and it makes them feel more comfortable than when people are dressed up in weird costumes. I'm disturbed by the reality of that; I find it darker when there's a light-hearted attitude to violence and it's more identifiable than when something is completely removed from reality. I've always had trouble understanding that, and I think at the end of the day, when the movie came out, it was a no-win situation. If the movie doesn't make the same amount of money or more, it's a disappointment. And they got a lot of flak from parents thinking it was too scary for their kids. So I think at the end of it all, I put them through the ringer too much.

But I will hang on to the third one, because I feel close to that material. I certainly don't feel like dissociating myself from the material completely because I feel I gave it something.

I'd like to carry on making movies, but I want to try to keep the same attitude I had when I first got into it. I had never consciously planned on being a director and so when I stumbled into it, it was a very surreal, wonderful experience. That's why I keep myself open; it was new and surreal and therefore exciting in a way. So whatever I need to do to keep that feeling, that's what I'll do.

Filmography

1982
Vincent
Producer: Tim Burton
Director: Tim Burton
Screenplay: Tim Burton
Cinematography (black and white): Victor Abdalov
Cast: Vincent Price (narrator)
5 mins. 16 mm

Seven-year-old Vincent Malloy fantasizes about being Vincent Price.

Hansel and Gretel
Executive producer: Julie Hickson
Director: Tim Burton
Screenplay: Julie Hickson
Cinematography: to come
Cast: Michael Yama, Jim Ishida
45 mins. 16 mm

A variation on the Grimms' fairy tale with an all-Asian cast.

Frankenweenie
Production company: Walt Disney
Producer: Julie Hickson
Director: Tim Burton
Screenplay: Lenny Ripp, based on an original idea by Tim Burton
Cinematography (black and white): Thomas Ackerman
Editor: Ernest Milano, A.C.E.
Music: Michael Convertino, David Newman
Art director: John B. Mansbridge

Cast includes: Shelley Duvall (Susan Frankenstein), Daniel Stern (Ben Frankenstein), Barrett Oliver (Victor Frankenstein), Joseph Maher (Mr Chambers), Roz Braverman (Mrs Epstein), Paul Bartel (Mr Walsh), Domino (Ann Chambers), Jason Hervey (Frank Dale), Paul C. Scott (Mike Anderson), Helen Bell (Mrs Curtis)
25 mins. 35 mm

Victor Frankenstein's dog, Sparky, chases a ball into the road and is hit by a car and killed. When Victor's teacher, Mr Walsh, shows his science class how electricity can be used to give life to a dead frog, Victor digs up his beloved pet from the local pet cemetery. He reanimates Sparky and keeps him out of sight in the attic. But Sparky sneaks out and terrifies the neighbours. When Mr Frankenstein discovers his son's secret he decides to invite everyone from the neighbourhood to the house to reintroduce them to Sparky. The evening descends into chaos and Sparky runs off to the local miniature golf course. Victor follows him there, along with an angry mob of neighbours. Sparky is killed saving Victor from a flaming windmill. The neighbours rally round and bring him back to life using jump leads attached to their car batteries. Revived, he finds romance with a poodle.

1984
Aladdin and his Wonderful Lamp
Production company: A Platypus Production in association with Lion's Gate Films
Executive producer: Shelley Duvall
Producer: Bridget Terry, Fredric S. Fuchs
Director: Tim Burton
Screenplay: Mark Curtiss, Rod Ash
Music: David Newman, Michael Convertino
Production designer: Michael Erler
Cast: Valerie Bertinelli (Princess Sabrina), Robert Carradine (Aladdin), James Earl Jones (Genie of the Lamp and Genie of the Ring), Leonard Nimoy (Evil Magician), Ray Sharkey (Grand Vizier), Rae Allen (Aladdin's Mother), Joseph Maher (Sultan), Jay Abramowitz (Habibe), Martha Velez (Lady Servant), Bonnie Jefferies, Sandy Lenz and Marcia Gobel (the Three Green Women), John Salazar (Servant)
47 mins. Colour video

Version of the classic tale shot for Shelley Duvall's *Faerie Tale Theatre* TV series.

1985
Pee-Wee's Big Adventure
Production company: Aspen Film Society-Shapiro/Warner Bros.
Executive producer: William E. McEuen
Producers: Robert Shapiro, Richard Gilbert Abramson
Director: Tim Burton
Screenplay: Phil Hartman, Paul Reubens, Michael Varhol
Cinematography (colour): Victor J. Kemper, A.S.C.
Editor: Billy Webber
Music: Danny Elfman
Production designer: David L. Snyder
Cast includes: Pee-Wee Herman (Himself), Elizabeth Daily (Dottie), Mark Holton (Francis), Diane Salinger (Simone), Judd Omen (Mickey), Irving Hellman (Neighbour), Monte Landis (Mario), Damon Martin (Chip), David Glasser, Gregory Brown, Mark Everett (BMX Kids), Daryl Roach (Chuck), Bill Cable, Peter Looney (Policemen), James Brolin (PW), Morgan Fairchild (Dottie)
90 mins. 35 mm

One day after breakfast, Pee-Wee Herman takes out his beloved red and white bicycle to admire it. Later, rich kid Francis offers to buy it from Pee-Wee, who refuses and rides into town to visit the local joke shop and pick up a new horn for his bike. When he returns to where he padlocked it, he discovers the bike has been stolen. The police can't help, so he consults a fortune-teller who (wrongly) informs him that his bike is in the basement at the Alamo.

Setting off to find his bike he hitches a ride with, firstly, an escaped convict and then Large Marge, a ghostly trucker, who died a year previously. She drops him off at a roadside diner where he is befriended by Simone, a waitress who dreams of visiting Paris. Pee-Wee encourages her to go and after being chased by Simone's jealous boyfriend eventually he makes it to the Alamo where he is horrified to discover there is no basement. Later, after riding a wild bull and wooing over a bar-room full of bikers with a dazzling version of 'Tequila', Pee-Wee has an accident and winds up in hospital where he sees his bike on TV being presented to a child-star for use in an forthcoming film. Rushing to the studio, Pee-Wee sneaks on to the lot, steals back his bicycle and is chased through various soundstages.

Having escaped, he spies a pet shop on fire and stops to rescue the animals from the blaze. Passing out in front of the store he is arrested. However, a studio executive is convinced Pee-Wee's story will make a great movie and turns his tale into a James Bond-style adventure with Pee-Wee cameoing as a hotel bell-hop. Later, everyone who Pee-Wee encountered during his quest turns up for the film's world premiere at the local drive-in.

The Jar
Director: Tim Burton
Screenplay: Michael McDowell from Ray Bradbury's original teleplay
Music: Danny Elfman
Cast: Griffin Dunne, Paul Bartel
23 mins.

Episode of the *Alfred Hitchcock Presents* TV series.

Family Dog
Cartoon TV series produced by Amblin for which Burton acted as executive producer as well as design consultant.

1988
Beetlejuice
Production company: The Geffen Company
Producers: Michael Bender, Larry Wilson, Richard Hashimoto
Director: Tim Burton
Screenplay: Michael McDowell, Warren Skaaren, story by Michael McDowell, Larry Wilson
Cinematography (colour): Thomas Ackerman
Editor: Jane Kurson
Music: Danny Elfman
Production designer: Bo Welch
Cast includes: Alec Baldwin (Adam Maitland), Geena Davis (Barbara Maitland), Jeffrey Jones (Charles Deetz), Catherine O'Hara (Delia Deetz), Winona Ryder (Lydia Deetz), Sylvia Sidney (Juno), Robert Goulet (Maxie Dean), Glenn Shadix (Otho), Dick Cavett (Bernard), Annie McEnroe

(Jane), Michael Keaton (Betelgeuse), Patricia Martinez (Receptionist), Simmy Bow (Janitor), Maurice Page (Ernie)
92 mins. 35 mm

Happily-married couple Adam and Barbara Maitland decide to spend their holiday decorating their idyllic New England home. Returning from a trip to town, Adam swerves to avoid hitting a dog. Their car dives off of a bridge into the river and they are killed. The couple arrive back at their house where a book entitled *Handbook for the Recently Deceased* reveals to them their predicament. Although they are now ghosts, they can remain in their home; if they try to leave, they end up in another dimension, a desert world populated by enormous sandworms.

Their peace is soon shattered, however, when their house is sold and the new residents arrive from New York. The Deetzes – henpecked Charles, would-be sculptor Delia and their morose daughter Lydia – under the guidance of obese interior designer, Otho, begin transforming the house into a horrific piece of modern art. The Maitlands seek help from their afterlife case worker, Juno, who informs them that they must remain in the house for 125 years, and if they want the Deetzes out, it is up to them to scare them away. But the Maitlands' attempt to haunt their home proves ineffectual. Although the Maitlands remain invisible to Charles and Delia, their daughter Lydia can see Adam and Barbara and becomes their friend.

Against the advice of Juno, the Maitlands contact the miscreant Betelgeuse, a freelance bio-exorcist, to scare away the Deetzes, but Betelgeuse is more interested in marrying Lydia and re-entering the real world. It takes the combined efforts of the Maitlands and Lydia to defeat Betelgeuse and banish him to the afterlife. The Deetzes and the Maitlands decide to live together in harmony.

1989
Batman
Production company: Warner Bros
Executive producers: Benjamin Melniker, Michael Uslan
Producers: Jon Peters, Peter Guber, Chris Kenney
Director: Tim Burton
Screenplay: Sam Hamm, Warren Skaaren, story by Sam Hamm, based on Batman characters created by Bob Kane
Cinematography (colour): Roger Pratt

Editor: Ray Lovejoy
Music: Danny Elfman
Production designer: Anton Furst
Cast: Jack Nicholson (Joker/Jack Napier), Michael Keaton (Batman/Bruce Wayne), Kim Basinger (Vicky Vale), Robert Wuhl (Alexander Knox), Pat Hingle (Commissioner Gordon), Billy Dee Williams (Harvey Dent), Michael Gough (Alfred), Jack Palance (Carl Grissom), Jerry Hall (Alicia). 126 mins. 35 mm

Gotham City is in the grip of mob boss Carl Grissom. Reporter Alexander Knox and photo-journalist Vicky Vale begin investigating the truth behind the rumours of a shadowy vigilante figure dressed as a bat, who has been terrifying criminals throughout the city.

Vale and Knox attend a benefit at the mansion of millionaire Bruce Wayne, who is taken by Vicky's charms. That same night, Grissom's second in command, Jack Napier, attempts to raid a chemical factory. When the police arrive, Napier realizes he's been set-up by his boss, angered by his affair with Grissom's girl. In the midst of the shoot-out, Batman arrives and Napier is tossed into a vat of toxic waste, later emerging hideously deformed as The Joker – his mouth twisted into a permanent grin, his face deathly white, his hair green.

After killing Grissom, The Joker takes over his empire and holds the city at his mercy by chemically altering everyday hygiene products so that those using a certain combination of products die. Batman, who is revealed to be Bruce Wayne's alter-ego, attempts to track down The Joker, who has become interested in Vicky Vale. The Joker, it turns out, killed Bruce's parents when he was a boy. The Joker holds a parade through Gotham, luring its citizens on to its streets by dispensing money, intending to kill them with a lethal gas. Batman foils his plan, but The Joker kidnaps Vicky and takes her to the top of Gotham Cathedral. After a fight with Batman, The Joker is thrown from the belfry, but his body is mysteriously absent from the ground below.

Beetlejuice: The Animated Series
Burton was executive producer of the Beetlejuice animated TV series.

1990
Edward Scissorhands
Production company: Twentieth Century Fox

Executive producer: Richard Hashimoto

Producers: Denise Di Novi, Tim Burton
Director: Tim Burton
Screenplay: Caroline Thompson, story by Tim Burton and Caroline Thompson.
Cinematography (colour): Stefan Czapsky
Editor: Richard Halsey, A.C.E.
Music: Danny Elfman
Production designer: Bo Welch
Special makeup and scissorhands effects: Stan Winston Studio
Cast includes: Johnny Depp (Edward Scissorhands), Winona Ryder (Kim), Dianne Wiest (Peg), Anthony Michael Hall (Jim), Kathy Baker (Joyce), Robert Oliveri (Kevin), Conchara Ferrell (Helen), Caroline Aaron (Marge), Dick Anthony Williams (Officer Allen), O-Lan Jones (Eseralda), Vincent Price (The Inventor), Alan Arkin (Bill)
105 mins. 35 mm

In a large, gothic-looking hilltop castle overlooking a pastel-coloured suburbia, Avon lady Peg Boggs finds Edward Scissorhands living all alone. The unfinished creation of an inventor who died of a heart attack before he could complete the job, Edward has everything a human should have, except, instead of hands, he has a pair of lethal shears. Feeling sorry for Edward, Peg removes him to her suburban home to live with her family.

Edward is soon accepted into the neighbourhood, revealing himself to be gifted at topiary and hairdressing. He is attracted to Peg's cheerleader daughter Kim, but she only has eyes for her brutish boyfriend, Jim, until he tricks Edward into helping him rob his parents' house and Edward is caught by the police and thrown in jail.

Later when Edward refuses the advances of Joyce, the local nympho-maniac, she turns the community against him, and he is chased to his mansion where he fights and kills Jim. Kim convinces everybody that Edward was also killed, leaving him alone in his castle once again.

Conversations with Vincent (working title)
Documentary about Vincent Price directed by Burton.

1992
Batman Returns
Production company: Warner Bros
Executive producers: Jon Peters, Peter Guber, Benjamin Melniker, Michael Uslan
Producers: Denise Di Novi, Tim Burton
Director: Tim Burton
Screenplay: Daniel Waters, story by Daniel Waters and Sam Hamm, based on Batman characters created by Bob Kane
Cinematography (colour): Stefan Czapsky
Editor: Chris Lebenzon
Music: Danny Elfman
Production designer: Bo Welch
Cast includes: Michael Keaton (Batman/Bruce Wayne), Danny De Vito (Penguin), Michelle Pfeiffer (Catwoman/Selina Kyle), Christopher Walken (Max Shreck), Michael Gough (Alfred), Michael Murphy (Mayor), Cristi Conway (Ice Princess), Andrew Bryniarski (Chip), Pat Hingle (Commissioner Gordon), Vincent Schiavelli (Organ Grinder), Steve Witting (Josh), Jan Hooks (Jen), John Strong (Sword Swallower), Rick Zumwalt (Tattooed Strongman), Anna Katarina (Poodle Lady), Paul Reubens (Penguin's Father), Diane Salinger (Penguin's Mother)
126 mins. 35 mm

A deformed baby boy is thrown into Gotham City's river by his horrified parents. Thirty-three years later, the child has been transformed into the hideous Penguin, whose gang disrupts the ceremonial lighting of Gotham's Christmas tree and kidnaps millionaire industrialist Max Shreck. Armed with evidence of the villainous Shreck's many crimes, the Penguin blackmails him into helping him discover the identity of his parents.

When The Penguin's plight becomes news, he's propelled into running for mayor. Batman is unconvinced by The Penguin, believing that he and his gang are responsible for several child murders. Meanwhile, Shreck hurls his dizzy secretary, Selina Kyle, from the top of his company's building when she discovers his plan to build a super power-plant and drain Gotham of its electricity.

Resuscitated by a group of cats, Selina returns home and after a quick bit of needlework emerges as Catwoman. Kyle, meanwhile, is being romanced by Batman's alter-ego Bruce Wayne, a situation complicated by Catwoman's teaming up with The Penguin in an effort to rid Gotham of

Batman. When Batman exposes The Penguin's nasty, demented, villainous ways, thereby ruining his political chances, the Penguin mounts an attack to kill all of Gotham's first-born infants. Batman foils his scheme and Catwoman, after killing Shreck, escapes to fight another day.

Singles
Burton cameos as Brian, a director of dating agency videos, in writer-director Cameron Crowe's movie.

1993
Tim Burton's The Nightmare Before Christmas
Production company: Touchstone Pictures
Producers: Tim Burton, Denise Di Novi
Director: Henry Selick
Screenplay: Caroline Thompson, based on a story and characters by Tim Burton, adaptation by Michael McDowell
Cinematography (colour): Pete Kozachik
Editor: Stan Webb
Music, lyrics and score: Danny Elfman
Art director: Deane Taylor
Cast: Danny Elfman (Jack Skellington's singing voice), Chris Sarandon (Jack's speaking voice), Catherine O'Hara (Sally), William Hickey (Evil Scientist), Glenn Shadix (Mayor), Paul Reubens (Lock), Catherine O'Hara (Shock), Danny Elfman (Barrel), Ken Page (Oogie Boogie), Ed Ivory (Santa)
76 mins. 35 mm

Fed up with Hallowe'en, Jack Skellington, the Pumpkin King of Hallowe'entown, discovers a doorway in the forest that leads to Christmastown. Enchanted by what he sees, Jack decides that next year he wants to run Christmas, and dispatches the mischievous trio Lock, Shock and Barrel to kidnap Santa. When Christmas Eve arrives, Jack takes off on his skeletal reindeer-driven sled to deliver the presents manufactured by the residents of Hallowe'entown, but instead of enchanting children the world over, the gifts terrify them. Eventually, Jack's sled is shot down by the police and he returns to Hallowe'entown. Santa is freed and order is restored.

Cabin Boy
Comedy directed by Adam Resnick and produced by Burton and Denise Di Novi for Touchstone Pictures.

1994
Ed Wood
Production company: Touchstone Pictures
Executive producer: Michael Lehmann
Producers: Tim Burton, Denise Di Novi
Director: Tim Burton
Screenplay: Scott Alexander, Larry Karaszewski_
Cinematography (black and white): Stefan Czaspsky
Editor: Chris Lebenzon
Music: Howard Shore
Production designer: Tom Duffield
Cast includes: Johnny Depp (Ed Wood) Martin Landau (Bela Lugosi), Sarah Jessica Parker (Dolores Fuller), Patricia Arquette (Kathy O'Hara), Jeffrey Jones (Criswell), G. D. Spradlin (Reverend Lemon), Vincent D'Onofrio (Orson Welles), Bill Murray (Bunny Breckinridge), Mike Starr (Georgie Weiss), Max Casella (Paul Marco), Brent Hinkley (Conrad Brooks), Lisa Marie (Vampira), George 'The Animal' Steele (Tor Johnson), Juliet Landau (Loretta King), Clive Rosengren (Ed Reynolds), Norman Alden (Cameraman Bill), Leonard Termo (Make-up man Harry), Ned Bellamy (Dr Tom Mason)

Hollywood 1952, aspiring movie director Edward D. Wood Jr works in the plant shop of a Hollywood studio by day and puts on plays with his theatre group, The Casual Company, by night. One day on the way home from an interview for a directing job, he meets his idol and former big-screen horror star Bela Lugosi trying out coffins in a mortuary. Ed convinces an exploitation movie producer to let him write and direct a movie about a sex change and casts his new-found friend Bela Lugosi in a small part. When the film, *Glen or Glenda* – in reality the story of a man (played by Wood) who likes to dress in women's clothing – proves less than successful, Ed and his friends are forced to raise the funds themselves for another feature, *Bride of the Monster*, again starring Bela Lugosi.

Late one night Ed receives a call from Bela asking for help and he turns up to find his friend on the floor of his home. Ed checks Bela into a hospital to cure him of his morphine addiction, but when the hospital discovers that

Bela has no insurance to pay for the treatment he is discharged.

Ed shoots a small amount of footage of Bela leaving his house just before he dies. Later Ed incorporates this footage into another movie, *Plan 9 from Outer Space*, the financing for which he raises from the Baptist church of Beverley Hills. *Plan 9*'s cast and crew, including Ed and his wife-to-be Kathy, attend the première. The couple leave for Las Vegas to get married immediately afterwards, with Ed convinced that *Plan 9* will be the film he will be remembered for.

James and the Giant Peach
Work began on a stop-motion animated film based on the story by Roald Dahl, directed by Henry Selick and executive produced by Burton and Di Novi for Touchstone Pictures.

1995
Batman Forever
A continuation of the Batman saga in which Batman (Val Kilmer) confronts The Riddler (Jim Carey). Directed by Joel Schumacher and executive produced by Tim Burton.

Bibliography

The Motion Picture Annual, 1986, 1989, 1991, 1993, Cine Books Inc.

Selected Interviews/Articles

Cinefex, no. 34, 1989
Premiere, vol. 2, no. 11, July 1989
Cinefantastique, vol. 20, no. 1/2, November 1989
Cinefex, no. 41, February 1990
Starburst, no. 155, July 1991
Cinefantastique, vol. 22, no. 2 October 1991
Cinefex, no. 51, August 1992
GQ (US), November 1993

Note on the Editor

Mark Salisbury was born in 1966 and is the author of two books, *The Making of Clive Barker's Nightbreed*, and *Behind the Mask: The Secrets of Hollywood's Monster Makers*. He has written for numerous publications in the UK and the US and is currently Features Editor for *Empire Magazine*.

Index

Numbers marked in bold type denote a chapter covering the subject
Page numbers in italics refer to illustrations